Heat of the Moment

Heat of the Moment

25 extraordinary stories from Olympic and Paralympic history

Edited by
Andrew Longmore

WILEY

Contents

3 Great Team Efforts

4 The Shadow of Munich

5 'Winners' in Defeat

6 Unexpected Drama

About the Editor

Andrew Longmore is an award winning writer on *The Sunday Times*, where he covers all the Olympic sports as well as football, cricket and racing. He has been Chief Sports Feature Writer at *The Times* and Chief Sports Writer at the *Independent on Sunday*, covering four Summer and three Winter Games, as well as football, rugby and cricket World Cups. Andrew's awards include Olympic Sports Reporter of the Year in 2000 and Sports Feature Writer of the Year in 2003. He has also writen several books including a biography of jockey Kieren Fallon.

Acknowledgements

The publishers would like to thank Marla Runyan for allowing use of extracts from her autobiography, *No Finish Line, My Life as I see it*, written with Sally Jenkins (Penguin USA, 2002) in 'Marla's Inner Vision' by Kate Battersby.

The publishers would like to thank the following for permission to reproduce the images in this book:

Plate section 1: 1© Getty Images; 2 © Getty Images; 3 © Getty Images: 4©Bongarts /Getty Images; 5 © Getty Images; 6 © AFP/Getty Images; 7 © Popperfoto / Getty Images; 8 © Getty Images; 9 © Getty Images; 10 © 2008 Bob Thomas / Getty Images; 11 © Getty Images; 12 © Getty Images; 13: © Bob Thomas /Getty Images.

Plate section 2: 14 © Getty Images; 15 © Getty Images; 16 © Popperfoto /Getty Images; 17 © AFP/Getty Images; 18 © AFP/Getty Images; 19 © Getty Images; 20 © Nick Wilson /Allsport / Getty Images; 21 © Popperfoto /Getty Images; 22 © Getty Images; 23 © AFP / Getty Images; 24 © Getty Images.

Introduction

The Ancient Greek word *athlos* or *athlon*, from which the word 'athlete' derives, means suffering as well as competing. To the Greeks, you could not have one without the other. 'No pain, no gain' in the modern phrase. The Olympic Games, ancient or modern, is the embodiment of pain and gain. Ask any athlete in any discipline and they will tell you that most of the four years of an Olympiad are spent in a state of mental and physical exhaustion. The gains, the winning of medals and cups and ultimately of Olympic gold medals, are fleeting in comparison. The Olympic and Paralympic Games in London 2012 will be, like all its predecessors, a celebration of human strength and an acknowledgment of human weakness. Or to put it into its rawest form, in the words of the British oarsman and double Olympic champion Steve Williams: 'There comes a point when you ask your body a simple question. Yes or no?'

The history of the Games, like the history of the world, is written by the winners. Yet, in the pages of this book, the losers have their moment too. Dorando Pietri, the little Italian who staggered across the line in the Marathon at the London 1908 Games only to be disqualified, became far more famous worldwide than the American, Johnny Hayes, the gold medallist. Pietri ended his days driving a taxi in San Remo, regaling his passengers with tales of his exploits. His memory has survived in Olympic folklore and in the name of an unremarkable street beneath which lies the finishing straight at the old White City track. Or take the remarkable American runner Marla Runyan, who would not let a simple matter like being certified blind hinder her Olympic ambitions. Runyan ran on feel rather than sight, but her senses let her down in the 1,500m at the Sydney 2000 Games and she broke for home too soon, fading in the closing stages. But what mattered more than defeat or victory was the lasting vision she created for other Paralympic athletes such as Oscar Pistorius, the Blade Runner from South Africa, whose triple gold at the Beijing 2008 Games is described so vividly by Kevin McCallum. Pistorius, who had both of his lower legs amputated at the age of 11 months, also intends to defy the laws of possibility by competing at the Olympic Games in London 2012. Kate Battersby's interview with Margaret Maughan, Britain's first Paralympic gold medallist, shows just how far disability sport has come in the last 50 years. In Rome 1960, Maughan, who competed in the Archery tournament, only knew she'd won a medal when she was summoned from the team bus to attend the ceremony several hours after the finish of her competition.

This is not intended to be a comprehensive chronicle of the Olympic Movement nor exclusively a compendium of champions. Equipment has changed along with the human form, methods of preparation, training techniques, times, speeds and rewards. Many athletes competing in the Games are funded well enough to train full time. The age of the part-time Corinthian has gone forever. But the essential emotions of the competition, the reaction to victory and defeat and the impossibly slim margins between the two, have remained remarkably unchanged since Athens hosted the first modern Olympic Games at the end of the nineteenth century. Ask Olympians what they fear most and it is the potential waste of time, the threat of training for four whole years, day after day, week after week, eating, sleeping and dreaming their sport only to come away with nothing.

Sir Steve Redgrave's journey to a fifth gold medal, overcoming serious illness on the way, is only part of the story retold by Nick Townsend. In the parentheses of Olympic history is Ed Coode, who had lost his place to Redgrave in the Fours only a few months before the Sydney 2000 Games. Coode raced instead with Greg Searle in the Pairs, the race before Redgrave's assault on history. They finished fourth and were devastated by their defeat. Unnoticed by the 11 million people back in Britain who stayed up into the early hours to watch Redgrave win, they receded into the background of the tableau, a forlorn counterpoint to the great victory march. The story, though, has a happy ending. Four years later, Coode himself was a late replacement in the Fours led by Matthew Pinsent at the Athens 2004 Games, which won gold by a few millimetres. Satisfied that he had settled an old score, Coode headed to the West Country to begin a new life as a country solicitor. Though 13,000 journalists now cover an Olympic Games, the abiding frustration of reporting it is the knowledge that a thousand stories have been left untold. Not even the camera can be everywhere.

The Olympic Movement itself has changed out of all recognition. It is now big business, a geopolitical as well as a sporting force in the world, capable of leaving a lasting legacy for Host Cities long after the Olympic Flame has been handed on. Just ask the people of Barcelona, who surprised everyone when they welcomed the Games in the summer of 1992 and introduced the world to a confident new Spain. Barcelona began the Games as the first city of Catalonia and the second city of Spain. Today, tourists still flock to its busy streets and marvel at the sweeping grandeur of its Olympic sites. Or take Sydney 2000, which, as Tom Knight recalls, hosted a Games that has become the model for the twenty-first century, a triumph for a vibrant new nation utterly committed to sporting excellence and its embodiment in the Olympic and Paralympic Games. Yet it's not the architecture or the politics that excites billions of people at every Olympic Games, it's the human theatre.

Where possible, in the 25 essays in *Heat of the Moment*, we have matched journalists to events they witnessed. There will be an element of hindsight to the drama now, but the passion still leaps from the pages of Neil Wilson's account of David Hemery winning the 400m Hurdles at the Mexico City 1968 Games, perhaps the single most extraordinary performance by a British track athlete in Olympic history, of Gareth A. Davies's remarkable story of how the Australian Wheelchair Basketball team overturned the odds at the Sydney 2000 Games and how the commentary by the BBC's Barry Davies of the closing stages of the GB Hockey team's epic victory over Germany in the final at the Seoul 1988 Games has become part of a legendary success. The 'moment' is key, the moment of triumph or defeat, elation or despair or, in the case of Marla Runyan, the moment of anticlimax. Sometimes the telling becomes part of the narrative.

Murray Hedgcock, reporting from the Munich 1972 Games, slipped into the Olympic Village as part of the Australian Basketball team to report on the hijack of 11 Israeli athletes only to find that he was better off outside watching television like every other journalist. Being close to the action does not always guarantee a reporter the best seat. Even in these days of mobile phones, the Internet and Twitter, there are still embarrassing moments when your sports desk knows more about an event 5,000 miles away than you do a mile down the road. My own experience of the GB 4 x 100m Relay gold in Athens 2004, one of the greatest of all upsets, came perilously close to farce in the aftermath of Kelly Holmes's second gold. One moment the double Olympic champion was sharing her moment of fulfilment with a roomful of journalists, the next she was talking to an empty room as news of the defeat of the crack American sprint squad by an out-of-sorts British quartet spread through the ranks. Typical, you wait 92 years for a men's Relay gold and it comes right out of the blue and right on deadline.

Paul Hayward's compelling recollection of Usain Bolt's world record 100m in Beijing 2008 echoes the shocked reaction of Tom Knight when Ben Johnson annihilated Carl Lewis in Seoul 1988. No one could believe what they had just seen in Seoul, quite rightly, as it proved, in Johnson's case. There is no attempt to hide the darker side of the Games or the fact that as the stakes rise so does the temptation to cheat. Johnson's disgrace prompted a fundamental change in the attitude of the whole Olympic Movement towards drug-taking. The notorious Berlin 1936 Games, organised to glorify the Nazi Party, proved a propaganda coup for the greatest of black American athletes, Jesse Owens. Craig Lord's brilliant essay on the lifelong friendship between Owens and Luz Long, a white German long jumper, which was first formed during their competition, confirms the eternal healing power of sport. When Long was killed in the Second World War, Owens continued to correspond with Long's family until his own death from lung cancer in 1980.

No one in Stadium Australia on that star-studded night in Sydney 2000 could have failed to be moved by the solitary figure of Cathy Freeman, the waif who ran the 400m with the entire Aboriginal people clinging to her back and then, sitting alone on the track in front of 80,000 people, realised the enormity of her achievement. Freeman did not crave celebrity or fame, she was frightened by the consequences of victory, but she understood the significance of the moment that memorable night in Sydney and ran for her life. Freeman, who also lit the Olympic Flame in Sydney, was recently described as a 'national institution' by the head of the Australian Olympic Committee and is now heavily engaged in charity work on behalf of disadvantaged Aboriginal communities. For Freeman, sport was always a means of expression; at the Olympic Games her eloquence reached every corner of a disparate land.

Inevitably, there are omissions. No Sebastian Coe or Steve Ovett, no Olga Korbut or Nadia Comaneci, no Michael Phelps or Mark Spitz, no Emil Zátopek, Lasse Virén or Haile Gebrselassie, no Derek Redmond, hobbling across the finishing line with a torn hamstring in the semi-final of the 400m in Barcelona, helped by his father and determined to complete the race and the journey he had begun many years before. No Daley Thompson, arguably the greatest British athlete of all time. Legitimate claims could be made for the inclusion of 100 other 'moments' and many other Games. But, with London 2012 fast approaching, it is instructive to reflect on the two previous London Games, in 1908 and 1948, one held in the last golden age before the onset of the First World War, the other as a desperate symbol of a return to peace and normality and, through them, to identify some common themes. Contrary to the perception of good-natured Corinthian sportsmanship, the 1908 Games were marred by dissent and mistrust between the Americans and the British, not the last time that two major powers would use the Games as a metaphor for global domination. Yet by the end of those Games, there was a firm structure in place to ensure their survival, one based on the primacy of National Olympic Associations and national governing bodies, and on the codification of rules for each and every sport.

London will host a spectacular Games, Olympic and Paralympic. By the end of it, a new series of images will have been created to chase away the past. Some will fade with time; others will endure, another stitch in the rich and complex tapestry of the Olympic and Paralympic Movements.

Andrew Longmore

'These are great moments
in the lives of individuals'

Jesse Owens, four times gold medallist
at the 1936 Olympic Games.

1
LANDMARKS OF HISTORY

London 1908: A Jewel in the Crown

Berlin 1936: '*Guten Morgen*, King George'

London 1948: The Games Revived

Sydney 2000: Lighting the Flame

A Jewel in the Crown

London 1908
Andrew Longmore

Built in less than a year, the White City was a proud monument to Edwardian design and an early icon of the Olympic Games

On a drab afternoon in an unfashionable suburb of west London in July 1908, the glitz and glamour of the modern Games was as distant as the skyline of the city. The rain had poured down all morning. The Stadium, newly built to host the Games, was only half full and a missing US flag had already caused the first flutter of discontent in the ranks of the competing nations.

Surveying the bedraggled scene below him, King Edward VII must have wondered whether his role as patron of the Games was quite fitting for a monarch, but he could hardly withdraw now, not with a host of the best athletes in the world gathered beneath him. 'I declare the Olympic Games of London open', said the king. The Grenadier Guards struck up the national anthem, the athletes gave three cheers and, at last, the sun came out as if to confirm that the Empire was still in safe hands.

If the start of the London 1908 Games proved rather low key, there was to be nothing routine about the competition that stretched out over the next three months.

For the first time, the Games included winter sports so – though the fortnight of the track and field, then as now, was the main attraction – the Ice Skating did not finish until October. Some 23 sports were included on the programme; most of them, such as Boxing, Sailing, Cycling, Fencing and Wrestling, remain central to the Games today. The oddities – Motor Boating (in Southampton Water), Lacrosse, Tug of War, Rackets – were added to the list mainly to boost the tally of the home team's medals. Perhaps the most bizarre spectacle of the whole Games was an exhibition of Bicycle Polo played across the vast infield of the White City Stadium.

Long before the competitors arrived in London, they knew that these Games were going to be different. No longer would it be possible for a passing tourist to win the gold medal, as had happened in the Tennis tournament at Athens in 1896, the first modern Olympics. Nor would local rules be applied randomly, as was often the case in Paris (1900) and St Louis (1904). Every one of the 2,023 competitors in the 1908 Games had to be registered with their Olympic Association and entered as a member of a national team. In London, athletes ceased to be talented amateurs, who took off their coats and ran, walked, cycled or swam to victory or defeat on their own, and became representatives of their people, flag-wavers, keepers of national pride. The amateur spirit was protected with zeal, but a corporate cloak was laid over the rampant individualism of the early Olympic years.

London should never have hosted these Games at all. Rome was the chosen venue until Mount Vesuvius erupted in 1906 and the fathers of the Eternal City asked to be relieved of the financial responsibility of hosting the Games. London came to the rescue and, in a remarkable tribute to the structure and organisation of sport in Edwardian England, completed preparations in less than two years. Indeed, the White City Stadium, the jewel in the crown of the 1908 Games, was designed and built in less than a year.

On the outside, the White City was a monument to great British design and engineering, confirmation, in 5,000 tonnes of steel, of the solidity of Britain's economic muscle. In fact, the project was masterminded by a Hungarian-born former circus performer called Imre Kiralfy, who had nursed his idea of a glowing White City, a confectionery of domes, palaces and bridges to be used as a backdrop for exhibitions, for 10 years before he came to England from his adopted home in America. When the idea for a Franco–British exhibition to cement the growing *entente cordiale* between the two nations was proposed, Kiralfy knew his dream could be realised at last.

A 567-hectare site near Shepherd's Bush was identified and a group of wealthy backers found to finance the scheme. As part of the exhibition complex – and, doubtless, to ingratiate himself in high society – Kiralfy offered to build the Stadium for the Olympic Games. A contract was signed with the newly created British Olympic Association, headed by Lord Desborough, and within 10 months a grand showpiece Stadium complete with separate tracks for Running and Cycling, and a 100m swimming pool dug into the infield, five 'temperance' restaurants, dressing-rooms for 3,000 athletes and facilities for ambulance and police services, had emerged white and shining from the industrial wasteland. The International Olympic Committee was delighted. A strong lobby had grown up to make Greece the permanent home of the modern

Olympic Games, but if London could finance and build such a grand Stadium inside a year, then so could future Host Cities. The Olympic Games could be portable. No one, though, could have foreseen the drama that would unfold within the massive acres of this new sporting wonder.

The success of a stadium, however, like any theatre, is not defined by its dimensions (seven Royal Albert Halls could fit inside the White City), but by the drama played out on stage. The fortnight of the track and field competition in 1908 produced more than its share of triumph and controversy, heroes and villains. The massive green acreage of the White City became the duelling ground for the two most powerful athletics nations in the world. For the 122-strong American team, the London 1908 Games was a precious chance to assert their superiority over their former colonial oppressors and to show the rest of the world their formidable strength on the sports field and, by extension, the battlefield. 'We will knock spots off the British', Martin Sheridan, the US team captain, had boasted before setting off from New York.

In contrast, the recent Boer War in South Africa had shown the British army to be inept and outdated and exposed a lack of fitness among the country's young men at just the moment that Germany was starting to flex its military muscles. While the underlying theme of the Olympic Movement was to bring nations together in peaceful competition, the attitude of the US team, belligerently led by James E. Sullivan (the head of the American Olympic Committee) and, to a lesser extent, of the hosts was closer to George Orwell's description of sport as 'war without the shooting'. Britain's manliness was under threat from across the Atlantic, as was her moral authority, her reputation for justice and fair play. Both had to be protected at all costs.

Ironically, Britain's determination to impose a structure onto the haphazard organisation of the Olympic Games only exacerbated the controversy. For the first time, qualifying standards were laid down and a set of rules for each of the 23 sports formulated and agreed by the majority of the competing nations (though not the USA, who did not attend the relevant meeting). Britain, in other words, was doing for Olympic sports what it had already done for football, cricket, hockey and tennis by codifying the rules and exporting them to the rest of the world.

The Americans were also looking to world sporting domination, not least in athletics, which they regarded as the true test of a nation's manhood. Sullivan, in fact, had travelled to England three years before the start of the London Games, well before London had even been allocated the event, to reach what he termed an 'athletic alliance' between America's Amateur Athletic Union and Britain's Amateur Athletic Association. Had he reached that accord, many of the controversies of the 1908 Games might have been avoided. He returned empty-handed, however, largely because the secretary of the AAA had an accident and had to be rushed to hospital. Unfortunately the Americans did not send a delegation to the spring 1907 IOC meeting in the Hague at which the rules and regulations for all the events were ratified, a mistake which also fostered many of the subsequent disagreements.

More than a century on, the disputes that raged through the fortnight of the track and field competition seem strange today. When the City of Liverpool Police team defeated the Americans with embarrassing speed in the Tug of War, the visitors raised an official objection to the 'specialist' hobnail boots worn by their opponents. The Liverpool team responded that these were not specialist boots at all, but normal police boots. The US objection was overruled and an offer by the Liverpool police team to replay the engagement without their boots was haughtily dismissed by the Americans.

Easily the most damaging of the controversies involved the American runner John Carpenter, who was penalised for impeding the British champion Lt Wyndham Halswelle, a Boer War veteran, in the final of the 400m. *The Times* reported the closing stages of the race the following day: 'Halswelle closed until almost even when the American who was next to him [Carpenter] began to run wide with the result that soon after Halswelle turned the bend he was forced very nearly onto the bicycle track.' With three Americans lined up against Halswelle, the fastest qualifier by nearly a second, in a race run without designated lanes, the British officials had been alerted to the probability of trouble and stationed themselves around the track. Before Carpenter crossed the line, an official had broken the tape, signifying 'no race'. After long deliberations by the all-British jury, Carpenter was disqualified and the race was rescheduled for the following afternoon. In protest, the remaining two American runners boycotted the rerun and Halswelle was left to complete the 400m in splendid isolation.

Having won 15 out of the 27 gold medals in track and field, the crack US team returned home in triumph, to a public parade through the streets of New York and a special reception hosted at his summer residence on Long Island by President Theodore Roosevelt, by no means the last politician to exploit the propaganda value of sporting success. But, by the end of a tumultuous summer, the organisers too thought the Games had been a success.

Lower ticket prices – and, presumably, news of the raging controversies – brought crowds of 65,000 to the White City for the second week of the Athletics and, for the first time, an Olympic Games made a small profit. Satisfyingly, Britain comfortably topped the overall medal table with 143 (56 golds), 97 more than the Americans, who did not field teams in many events. A clean sweep of the medals for women's Archery was not surprising because only the British team entered, but from the Rowing at Henley to the Boxing, Tennis and Shooting, Britain remained dominant. Britain also produced one of the individual stars of the Games in Henry Taylor, who won three gold medals in the increasingly muddy and churned up waters of the swimming pool.

Evolving from the early events in Paris and St Louis came the relative order of the London 1908 Games. But basing the organisational structure of the Olympic Games on national teams also encouraged the rise of a flag-waving nationalism, which led, inevitably, to the Berlin 1936 Games and the Cold War boycotts of Los Angeles and Moscow. The Americans certainly showed the Host Nation the way in terms of properly preparing and funding a sports team, but it was a while before Corinthian idealism was replaced by pragmatic professionalism in British sport. As a result of US protests, officials for future Games were no longer recruited from the Host Nation, but were independent, though exploiting home advantage is still regarded as a natural right of the Host Nation – up to a point.

The White City suffered a chequered career after the First World War. It never quite found its niche in the sporting market, although it became the home of greyhound racing and of the Amateur Athletics Association. It also hosted a match in the 1966 World Cup, almost its last hurrah as a major sports stadium. In 1984 the stadium was demolished: only a plaque where the finishing line used to be and a medal table etched in stone now mark the site of the first purpose-built Olympic Stadium. The rest of the White City lies buried beneath the BBC Television Centre and its offices on the west side of Wood Lane, just north of Shepherd's Bush. The memories are confined to the names of the surrounding streets. Australia Road, Commonwealth Avenue and Dorando Close, which runs diagonally towards Westway and traces almost exactly the home straight down which Dorando Pietri staggered to victory in the Marathon, only to be disqualified for receiving outside assistance. The legacy of the White City, however – a state-of-the-art stadium and forerunner of the futuristic structures that grace the modern Olympic complex – has survived intact.

'Guten Morgen, King George'

Berlin 1936
John Goodbody

*The brilliance of Jesse Owens became an enduring symbol
of the resilient spirit of the Olympic Games*

Jesse Owens once described the sense of terror that overcame him at the start of the 100m in Berlin. 'It's a nervous, terrible feeling,' he said. 'You feel as if you can't
carry the weight of your body. Your stomach isn't there,
your mouth is dry and your hands are wet with perspira-
tion. You know it will all be over in 10 seconds. These are
great moments in the lives of individuals.'

Owens' greatness was forged over six days in the
Olympic Stadium in Berlin in 1936. Here he won four gold
medals, but his name has echoed way beyond the bound-
aries of sport. He is not only one of the most celebrated athletes in history, but also the first Olympic sportsman to have
become an international symbol of his race. As an African
American, Owens' performances at the Berlin Games in
1936 were the perfect riposte to the Nazis, who unasham-
edly and to a greater extent than any other regime before
or since, had used the prestige of the Olympic Games as
a propaganda tool. For many Germans, however, Jesse
Owens was an idol: whenever he left the Olympic Village
he was mobbed by people demanding autographs.

Nazi ideology was founded on Aryan supremacy. Now, in their own heartland, Owens' victories in the 100m and 200m, 4 x 100m Relay and Long Jump had demonstrated to the world the falsity of the theory that black people were inferior. His supreme status in sport continued after his death. Even in 1984, when Los Angeles staged the Olympic Games, Carl Lewis summoned the ghost of J.C. 'Jesse' Owens in his quest to win four gold medals and duplicate the performance of his legendary predecessor. For many years Owens set the standard for the measurement of excellence.

Not particularly tall or muscular at 1.78m tall and 71kg, Owens had been inspired to become a sprinter when in 1928 he met Charlie Paddock, known as 'The Golden Streak from the Gold West' and the 100m champion of the Antwerp 1920 Games. In the heats of the 100m in Berlin, Owens equalled the Olympic record of 10.3 and then cruised through the semi-final. In the final, he defeated his great rival Ralph Metcalfe, another black athlete. In the 200m Final, held in light rain, Owens won in 20.7, some 4m clear of a third black sprinter, Mack Robinson. It was no wonder that when Owens returned to the US after the Games, he was given a ticker-tape parade down Broadway, though – and Owens never forgot it – he was not sent a telegram of congratulation by the president, Franklin D. Roosevelt.

Other Olympic Games have generated controversy before or while they have been held. In the case of the Berlin 1936 Games, however, the controversy has continued until the present day. People are still wondering what would have happened if those Games had been boycotted or even withdrawn from Berlin. Would such actions have influenced subsequent diplomatic attitudes in the

1930s? Would the Second World War have broken out as it did?

It has needed all the exploits of Owens, the hero of the Games, as well as those of many other outstanding competitors, to recognise that the Berlin 1936 Games were also a sporting contest. Their sporting quality remained despite the blatant promotion of the host country, Nazi Germany, and its fascist philosophy. As Dorothy Tyler, the last living British medallist from those Games recalls: 'We woke every morning to the sound of marching feet. When I got to the window, I could see young people with shovels, held like rifles on their shoulders. I learned they were the Hitler Youth. When we went shopping, we were greeted with 'Guten Morgen, Heil Hitler'. We replied: 'Guten Morgen, King George'. Tyler, then 16 years old, came second in the High Jump, an event for which German athlete Gretel Bergmann was not selected because she was Jewish. Josef Goebbels, Hitler's Propaganda Minister, had seized the opportunity of hosting the Games to promote Nazi Germany, realising its benefit for the martial solidarity of his countrymen. As he said: 'German sport has only one task: to strengthen the character of the German people, imbuing it with the fighting spirit and the steadfast camaraderie necessary for the struggle for its existence.'

Yet initially the Nazis had been indifferent, even hostile, to the event, which had been awarded to Berlin in 1931, two years before they came to power. Hitler dismissed it as an 'invention of Jews and Freemasons' and remarked they were a sort of 'Judaistic Theatre ... that cannot be put on in a Reich ruled by National Socialists.' Goebbels, more responsive to the power of the Olympic ideal, persuaded Hitler of the benefits of an Olympic Games. Gradually his enthusiasm increased, although there were quickly difficulties, particularly in relation to the Jews, against whom action became more and more repressive as the Games approached. The wife of Carl Diem, one German member of the International Olympic Committee (IOC), was Jewish, for example, and he himself was attacked by the Nazi media for being 'a white Jew'. Another half-Jewish German IOC member, Theodor Lewald, was moved from active organisation into the titular position as President of the Organising Committee. The post ended after the Games, but it did maintain some status to satisfy the IOC. The Nazi regime had learned that the IOC could only be pushed so far.

Although the Nazis confirmed that non-Aryans would be allowed to compete for Germany in 1936, their opportunities for any serious preparation were restricted since they were excluded from sports clubs. The imposition in 1935 of the Nuremburg Laws, which stated that Jews were subhuman, aroused particularly strong feelings in the USA, where a boycott movement was gaining momentum. In December 1935 the Amateur Athletic Union, which oversaw amateur sports in the country, only voted by a majority of three (out of 114) to send a team to Berlin. The most influential figure supporting the boycott was an American IOC member, Ernest Jahncke, and for his pains he was expelled from the IOC.

At the Winter Games in Garmisch-Partenkirchen preceding the Summer Games in 1936, Hitler received a rare rebuff. The IOC President, Henri de Baillet-Latour of Belgium, saw a sign outside a set of lavatories on the Olympic site, stating 'No dogs or Jews'. He protested to Hitler, only to be told an invited guest did not tell the host how to behave. Baillet-Latour retorted: 'Excuse me, Mr. Hitler, but when the Olympic flag is raised over the arenas, it is no longer Germany but Olympia and in Olympia we are the masters.' The signs were promptly taken down. Hitler's attendance at Garmisch-Partenkirchen demonstrated his personal commitment to the far more lavish Summer Games, scheduled to open on 1 August. The Olympic Stadium (still in regular use) was expanded to hold 110,000 people, and other magnificently appointed venues were put up under the direction of Albert Speer. The Nazis also commissioned a film to be made of the Games by the director Leni Riefenstahl. *Olympia* was to be the first of many subsequent films but it remains the most famous, with its graphic photography and portrayal of events such as the Pole Vault. Particularly striking is the start of the Torch Relay, with the lighting of the Flame at Olympia followed by its transport across Europe. The Torch Relay was introduced in 1936, and has subsequently become a feature of the Olympic and Paralympic Games.

Many members of the German team prepared for up to 12 months in training camps, and it showed. After taking only three gold medals in 1932, they were to get 40 just four years later. One competitor who did not train with her fellow team members was Helene Mayer; her father was a Jew and her membership of the Offenbach Fencing Club had been cancelled for racial reasons. Mayer, fifth in the Foil at the 1932 Games, was studying at a college in California. Perhaps because she was blonde and tall, as well as based in the United States, Mayer became an example of the Nazi's apparent inclusion of Jews in the German team. Although Mayer had had her citizenship withdrawn, she competed in Berlin, finished second, gave the Nazi salute on the podium and then returned to the United States, unhappy that her citizenship was not to be restored.

If the Jews were the domestic target of Nazi racism, then black athletes were the international target. The attitude of their Nazi hosts can be summed up in the words of Baldur von Schirach, leader of the Hitler Youth, who remarked: 'The Americans should be ashamed of themselves for letting their medals be worn by negroes. I myself would never shake hands with one.' However, it is almost certainly not true that Hitler specifically refused to shake hands with them because he also failed to greet many white athletes. There were 10 black athletes in the American track team of 60 and they won seven gold, three silver and one bronze medal. However, there was no questioning who was the star: Jesse Owens with his four titles in six days.

Owens and his contemporary and friend Joe Louis, who had just won the World Heavyweight Boxing title, were beacons of hope for black people in America. The youngest of 10 children and the grandson of a slave, Owens was born in Alabama in the 'Deep South' then moved to Ohio in the Midwest with his family. His athletic ability was shown early when he was long jumping almost 7m at the age of 15. At Ann Arbor, Michigan, on 25 May 1935, Owens had what has subsequently been known as his 'day of days'. In little more than three quarters of an hour, he broke five world records and equalled a sixth, with his long jump mark of 8.13m lasting for 24 years.

Owens won the 100m on 3 August 1936, defeating his fellow American Ralph Metcalfe, who had been the silver medallist four years earlier. When once asked about how he managed to run so fast, Owens replied: 'I let my feet spend as little time on the ground as possible.' The next day was the Long Jump, for which he was clear favourite – except that he nearly did not even qualify for the final. Owens did not realise that when he completed his final run-through, the competition had already started. Then, his second attempt was a foul because he had overstepped the take-off board. Then began perhaps the most famous friendship in Olympic history. The German Luz Long came across to Owens and, ignoring the racist tenets of his country's rulers, recommended that he move back his starting marker on the run-up to ensure that he qualify. This Owens did, although his third and final leap only qualified him by a centimetre. When, after an epic duel, Owens won the gold medal ahead of Long, with Hitler looking on, Long went across to shake the American's hand. The pair began chatting, starting a friendship that lasted until Long was killed in the Second World War. Owens went on writing to Long's family until he himself died in 1980 from lung cancer, caused by decades of smoking.

Everywhere one looked in 1936, there was evidence of the rise of the fascist powers. In the Marathon, the Koreans – gold-medallist Kee-Chung Sohn and bronze-medallist Seung-Yong Nam – were forced to represent Japan, then occupying their country, and to use Japanese names. Some 52 years later in Seoul, Sohn carried the Olympic Torch into the Stadium, finally able to celebrate both the victory of 1936 and his pleasure that his independent country could host the Olympic Games.

Few races engendered more excitement than the 1,500m. It pitched Jack Lovelock of New Zealand against Luigi Beccali of Italy, the defending champion, and Glenn Cunningham, 'The Iron Man of Kansas' – so called because he had been so badly burnt as a child in a fire, in which his brother died, that he was forced to recuperate in bed for two years, and his body remained scarred.

Lovelock, a student at Oxford and so virtually adopted as an Englishman, produced a scintillating last lap, cheered on by the BBC commentator Harold Abrahams, who shouted into his microphone 'Come on Jack'. Abrahams, the gold medallist in the 100m in the Paris 1924 Games, was equally enthusiastic when Britain defeated the United States in the 4 x 400m Relay. The victory was achieved without excessive preparation. As Godfrey Rampling, the longest living member of the quartet who died in 2009 aged 100, recalled: 'I remember saying one day "Look here chaps, we ought to practise some baton-changing." But we soon got bored and packed it in.'

The Rowing was dominated by Germany, who won all the finals, with the exception of the Double Sculls. Here, Britain's Dick Southwood and Jack Beresford, already winner of four medals including two golds at previous Games, were victorious. The Germans started before the umpire said 'Go', but were not recalled; the Britons, although 1½ lengths down at 1,000m, caught the Germans who eventually finished six seconds behind. For fortitude in overcoming a physical handicap, few could match the performance of Hungarian Olivér Halassy, who took a gold medal in the Water Polo to add to the gold he won in 1932 and the silver in 1928, despite having lost one leg when it was crushed by a tram when he was 11 years old. Halassy also won the 1931 European 1,500m Freestyle title. He was shot dead by a Soviet soldier in 1946.

Another display of fortitude came from the German rider Konrad von Wangenheim, who cracked a collarbone when he fell during the steeplechase in the Three-Day Equestrian event. He remounted and finished the course to ensure that his team was not disqualified. During the

Jumping event the next day he again fell, this time with the horse on top of him. Once more he remounted to help Germany to win the title.

Everywhere in 1936 there was a sense of unease, even foreboding, as the Games ended. When Henri de Baillet-Latour attended a dinner, a female neighbour at the table commented on the peaceful and harmonious conduct of the Games. 'Madam, may God preserve you from your illusions,' the President of the IOC apparently answered. 'If you ask me, we shall have war within three years.'

The Games Revived

London 1948

Nick Townsend

Amid hardship and post-war austerity, the Olympic Games brought a precious glimpse of international fellowship

Wembley Stadium, Saturday 7 August, on the eighth and final day of the London 1948 Athletics programme. Late on a searing afternoon already emotion-stoked by high achievement and gallant failure, the crowd could have been expected to make for home.

Few did, even at the end of a day in which they had already witnessed Fanny Blankers-Koen, the phenomenal all-rounder, secure a Relay gold – the last of four medals at these Games for the 30-year-old mother of two, known as the 'Flying Dutch housewife' – and the culmination of a Marathon that would leave a profound impression on all those present as they followed every faltering step of the Belgian Etienne Gailly on his agonising journey to the line. Some similarly tortured souls, such as Stan Jones, a British teacher, who was last of the 30th Marathon finishers but who departed with some kind of consolation that he was the final runner to tread the 1948 Olympic track, were still making their way into Wembley as the women's High Jump reached its denouement. No fewer than 65,000 spectators stayed on to witness an Olympic event that was to bring together, in very different ways, two remarkable women.

In those pre-celebrity days when initials rather than the informality of first names were the order, the 19 entrants had been distilled down to two finalists: Mrs D. Tyler of Great Britain and Miss A. Coachman, described by the British press as an 'American Negress'. Those vast thousands who had stayed behind would be present at an epoch-making moment in Olympic history as the two women engaged in 'one of the most thrilling duels imaginable', according to Harold Abrahams.

Dorothy Tyler and Alice Coachman both cleared 1.68m, a new Olympic record, but the pair then both failed in their three attempts at 1.7m. Tyler would later recall that her bra strap broke as she ran towards the bar on her last attempt, affecting her concentration – 'If it wasn't for that bra I might have won gold'. Coachman, who had cleared the final height on her first attempt, prevailed on a countback of jumps. However, the magnanimous Tyler, it was reported in the *Guardian*: 'snatched herself up from the sand after her last attempt and ran smiling to congratulate her opponent. Hers was the true spirit of sportsmanship which has governed all the events here.'

Alice Coachman received her medal from King George VI, the patron of the BOA who had also opened the Games, in the knowledge that she had become the first African-American woman to win gold in a track and field event. What made her feat all the more extraordinary was that the woman from Georgia in America's South had achieved it despite being barred from public sports facilities because of her race. She also lived in a society that discouraged women's involvement in sports. Never mind jumpers for goalposts, hers was a world of total improvisation in her training. She ran barefoot on dirt roads and in fields near her home in Albany and practised jumping over tied rags, ropes and sticks. She would almost certainly have won more medals had the 1940 and 1944 Games taken place. Coachman returned home as inspirational a figure for those who would follow her as Jesse Owens had been at the Berlin 1936 Games.

Coincidentally Tyler, a 28-year-old mother of two from Mitcham and the first female 'star' of British athletics, had observed Hitler's pre-war Germany from unusually close quarters. Her 1948 silver was a repeat of her achievement in 1936, when as 16-year-old Miss Odam, wearing homemade shorts and vest, she had finished runner-up in Berlin – beating Blankers-Koen into sixth in the process. She became the first British woman to win an Olympic medal there, all to a backdrop of Nazi flags and with the Hitler Youth heavily in evidence. Tyler had even been invited to a party organised by Hitler and Goebbels.

During the war Tyler had worked as a PT instructor and had also been a driver at military bases around Britain. Now, 12 years on from Berlin, her experiences encapsulated an event that from the outset bore the epithet the 'Austerity Games'. Initially, she hadn't even been on the list to compete, but in the spring of 1948 and just two months after the birth of her second son Tyler began training again. She revealed, though, that she had little time to do so and, having no coach, had to hone her technique without any help. The newspapers revelled in her story, and there were articles about how doing housework kept her fit. It was something she always denied, claiming she didn't do housework! What was true, however, was that in 1948 women had to make their own kit, on to which they sewed red, white and blue ribbons. Such was the state of Britain just three years after the end of the Second World War. The nation was still under strict rationing, far from ideal for an athlete. Tyler recalled many years later that she received an extra ration card and tinned fruit from Canada. She also sent her husband, Dick, to the butcher because 'they gave more meat to male customers'.

Despite all this, Tyler viewed the London 1948 Games as 'wonderful for the country', and quoted Emil Zátopek (the outstanding Czech distance runner, who won gold and silver at London 1948 and would proceed to claim gold at 5,000m, 10,000m and the Marathon at Helsinki 1952) who said, 'It was like the sun coming out after the terrible days of war'. Tyler added some perspective with her comment, 'The Games made a nice distraction from real life, but you didn't make it a priority.' Real life for most had involved contributing to Britain's rebuilding and regeneration after the destruction of war.

For that reason, London had not been the logical venue for the first post-war Olympic Games. The scarred capital was still recovering from the Luftwaffe's assault, which destroyed a million homes in the 76 consecutive days and nights of the Blitz. A number of American cities and those of neutral countries in the war could have staged the Games more easily, but London was regarded as a highly appropriate choice – symbolising, as it did, the restoration of freedom from Nazi tyranny. The driving force behind the decision was a Swede, J. Sigfrid Edström, the President of the IOC. It was to prove a wise choice.

Preparations were completed in barely more than two years, with what could be described as a 'make do and mend' approach. No new venues were constructed. Wembley, originally opened in 1923 for the British Empire

Exhibition, had to be converted from what it had become – a greyhound stadium – into an international track and field venue. There was no Olympic Village, as such, though many male athletes were accommodated in an Olympic Games Centre in Richmond Park. Huts originally built for army recruits in 1938 were dusted down and kitted out. The women stayed at schools and colleges; many of them at Southlands College, Wimbledon. The competitors travelled on the Underground or buses or were driven to the venues in the 'transport fleet' operated by the Women's Royal Voluntary Service. There were food contributions from nations including Holland, Denmark and Czechoslovakia. It would have been an affront to a nation still on rationing, undergoing peacetime stringency and rebuilding infrastructure, if the outlay had been lavish. The London 1948 Games, sandwiched between those of pre-war Berlin and those of Helsinki 1952 when the USSR and other Communist-bloc countries joined in, cost £750,000 (worth £80m today) and made a small profit.

Given the circumstances in which the Games had been organised, the Opening Ceremony could not have failed to be an uplifting occasion for the 80,000 who thronged to Wembley, though today there would undoubtedly have been controversy over the selection of the final Olympic Torchbearer into the Stadium. Sydney Wooderson, the retired British miler nicknamed 'The Mighty Atom', a man who had run the fastest mile in 1937, had been expected to carry the Torch from Olympia into Wembley. It was regarded as a fitting selection. But Wooderson, a solicitor, was slightly-built and bespectacled. Instead John Mark, an athlete who had not even made the British team, was named. Mark, a medical student and President of Cambridge University Athletic Club, happened to be tall and handsome and apparently he epitomised youthful vigour. For many, the choice, albeit unintentionally, was unfortunate in that it appeared to have echoes of Hitler's 'Aryan ideal' of the Berlin 1936 Games.

That apart, these Games emphasised how much the world had altered politically, socially and culturally since the 1930s. It was to be an Olympic Games of many 'firsts'. It saw the first political defection, of Marie Provaznikova, the 57-year-old Czechoslovakian President of the International Gymnastic Federation. It was also the first Games to be filmed in colour, and the first to be televised.

There had been limited television coverage at Berlin via closed circuit. But now, here in 1948, the BBC transmitted events live from Wembley, although admittedly broadcasting was still in its infancy and the number of television sets owned was limited. The Corporation's 64 hours of viewing, led by main commentators Richard Dimbleby and Wynford Vaughan-Thomas, was watched by an estimated audience of 500,000. The coverage, provided by two mobile TV units each carrying three cameras, proved so successful that on one day the broadcast was extended to seven and a half hours.

The major broadcasting hub of the London Games was the Radio Centre at the Palace of Arts in Wembley, which not only provided links to all 30 of the venues and serviced 200 foreign correspondents, but received the live television feeds as well. A fleet of specially adapted Humber Super Snipes carried the equipment for the Outside Broadcast Units, bringing live radio coverage back to the studios where the Games had to compete with *Woman's Hour* and *Music While You Work* for airtime. In addition, an Olympic film, the first to be filmed in colour, was out on general release less than two weeks after the end of the Games, the result of a £25,000 exclusive rights deal with J. Arthur Rank.

The events at Wembley attracted enthusiastic crowds who relished the spectacle of such characters as Zátopek. He was cheered on stirringly as he strove for 10,000m gold in that idiosyncratic anguished manner of his, head lolling and features contorted. Zátopek was one of 4,071 competitors from 59 nations participating (they did not include Germany and Japan, which were under Allied military occupations). After a 12-year hiatus, the first post-war generation was taking on the pre-war veterans, many of whom had undergone harrowing wartime experi-ences. One was the Belgian Marathon runner, Gailly, who had escaped from his German-occupied nation in 1943 and by a circuitous and hazardous route arrived in England, becoming a member of the Belgrave Harriers before taking part in the 1944 Airborne landings. He had been the first to enter the Wembley tunnel with just a circuit to complete. However, the long slope up the Olympic Way had drained the life out of a man who had never run a Marathon before, and whose engine was already running on vapour. *The Guardian* reported how the exhausted athlete, 'tottered like a man who had been dazed in the desert and knows that a few minutes away is water, blessed water', knowing 'he must carry Belgium's colours to the appointed end even if he fell and died in his track.' He was on that last pitiless circuit for four minutes, but held on to the bronze behind the Argentine Delfo Cabrera and the runner-up, Britain's Tom Richards.

Richards' silver was one of 23 medals won by British athletes. There had been no lofty expectations as the Second World War and its aftermath had severely restricted training and preparation. The hosts' three golds were won by Richard 'Dickie' Burnell and Bertram 'Bert' Bushnell in the men's Rowing Double Sculls, William 'Ran' Laurie (father of actor Hugh) and John 'Jack' Wilson in the men's Coxless Pairs and the sailors David Bond and Stewart Morris in the men's Swallow class. Amongst Britain's other medallists was 'Tebbs' Lloyd Johnson who, having competed since 1920, won a bronze in the 50k Walk. At 48, he was the oldest medal-winning athlete.

At one time on that final day at Wembley, the British tally did appear to have increased to four golds when a US athlete in the Relay was adjudged to have overrun the mark at the first change, prompting his quartet to be disqualified from first place. The verdict was overturned three days later, and the British athletes had to hand their medals back.

Of a total British contingent of 313 athletes, only 47 were women who contested nine events. In fact, the British women performed well, winning four silvers. Three of these could have been gold, but for the participation of Blankers-Koen who won the 100m, 200m and 80m Hurdles as well as securing gold in the Relay. But medals, of any hue, were of less importance than the Games' part in the process of Britain's post-war renewal and the return to a kind of normality. Considering the necessary economies involved, what was achieved in a matter of only two years was a testimony to British ingenuity and organisational prowess. As IOC president Edström was to reflect, 'The great test was taken and the organisation rose gloriously to the supreme challenge.'

Lighting the Flame

Sydney 2000

Tom Knight

The Opening Ceremony that lit up the world heralded a golden Games that set new standards for the 21st century

Framed by the cascading waterfall and dressed in a glistening white bodysuit, Cathy Freeman walked across the shimmering pond before turning, holding the torch high above her head and grinning nervously. While she gazed out at the thousands of flashbulbs sparkling in the night sky inside Stadium Australia, the cheers and whistles of the 110,000-strong crowd reflected their sheer delight at a special moment in the nation's history and their joy at the way in which the best kept secret of the Sydney 2000 Games was finally exposed.

No one in the Stadium or among the billions watching on television had expected the poster girl of these Games to be the athlete chosen to light the Olympic Cauldron that would herald the start of the Games of the XXVII Olympiad and the first of the Millennium. Yet, there she stood, in a fireproof full bodysuit, smiling at the surprise she had sprung. Freeman, after all, was under more pressure than any Australian competitor if the country was to make good on the prediction of John Coates, the team's

Chef de Mission, that it would achieve a top-five finish in the medals table. As the World Champion, she was odds-on favourite to win the 400m in the second week of the Games and surely, it was thought, she would not want her preparations compromised by this most public of duties. Freeman thought otherwise. This was the Olympic and Paralympic Games billed as 'the athletes' Games', and she was going to be there for the show-stopping start.

There had been many spectacular opening cere-monies, but this was one to savour. This was a truly daz-zling event, with Australia's most famous athlete seem-ingly walking on water to reach the middle of that pond at the foot of a bubbling torrent. Accompanied by the rous-ing choral surges of composer Hector Berlioz's *Te Deum*, Freeman bent slightly and pointed the Torch at the edge of the pond, igniting the first of the 150 jets that would spark into life as a ring of fire erupted from the irides-cent water. Fire and water; the image and the message was clear, for every Australian, the watching world and an Olympic Movement so keen for these Games to be suc-cessful. It was as spectacular as it was beautiful and the magic did not end there.

Amid questions about how it was all possible and the method by which Freeman would escape this burning cir-cle, the Sydney Symphony Orchestra reached yet another crescendo and with water dripping from below, the ring of fire that was the Olympic Cauldron slowly rose above Freeman's head. Only when Freeman was able to walk free from the flames did things begin to go wrong.

Instead of making its steady progress towards the top of the Stadium, the Cauldron jolted and then stopped in its tracks. The orchestra played on as Freeman shivered in the darkness, listening through her earpiece to the frantic cries of ceremony organisers as they realised that the technology had let them down. Writing in her autobiography, Freeman recalls the moment when calamity reigned. 'I'm just soaking wet, my legs are shaking violently and there are billions of people around the world staring at me right now. Three seconds later, I heard a series of men's voices in the earpiece all speaking over each other … I tried not to laugh because there was a cameraman right next to me. I figured there must be something wrong with the Cauldron.'

Long since edited out of television broadcasts of the event, the delay lasted some four minutes before the technical hitch was fixed and the relief was palpable when the Cauldron resumed its two-minute ascent to the top of the Stadium. Even with the glitch, this Opening Ceremony had been a masterpiece and, with the Cauldron safely installed to burn for the next 16 days, Freeman was finally able to find a jacket to cover her shivering body. It was only after the Olympic Games that she confessed to having a worrying cold in the few days before, though not even that would have prevented her from playing her part.

Freeman made her way down the five flights of steps to the track to meet for the first time the five athletes who had carried the Torch inside the Stadium and, fittingly, on the anniversary marking 100 years of women's participation in the Games, they were all very special women in Australian sport. As Tina Arena sang 'The Flame', Betty Cuthbert, the original 'Golden Girl' after her record haul of four gold medals from Melbourne 1956 and Tokyo 1964, was the first Torchbearer to enter the Stadium. As a multiple sclerosis sufferer, she was pushed in a wheelchair by Raelene Boyle, the sprint star from Mexico City 1968 and Munich 1972. They handed the Torch to Swimming

legend Dawn Fraser, who epitomised the Australian lar-
rikin spirit. She passed it on to the 75-year-old Shirley
Strickland de la Hunty, the sprint Hurdler, who won seven
medals in three Olympic Games. Swimmer, Shane Gould,
who in Munich was the only woman to win five individual medals and once held all the Freestyle world records
between 200m and 1,500m, handed the Torch to Debbie
Flintoff-King, the 400m Hurdles champion in Seoul 1988.

That it was Freeman who provided the climactic lighting of the Cauldron had come as a complete surprise
since even at the final rehearsal, in the early hours of the
day of the Opening Ceremony, her identity was kept from
all the Torchbearers apart from Flintoff-King – and then
only because the pair were collected from their city centre hotels by the same car in what was a highly secretive
operation. Freeman had even walked into the Stadium
with the Australian team, but none of the athletes noticed
when she slipped away to change into that unforgettable
bodysuit.

So it was that the Sydney organisers pulled off their stunning *pièce de résistance* with Freeman. Like so much of what
happened in the Sydney 2000 Olympic and Paralympic
Games, the Torch Relay was a triumph of planning and
execution, carried out with a friendliness and community
spirit well known in Australia. Until the beginning of the
year, the Games had been plagued by problems highlighted by the intense media scrutiny in the country.

One of them centred on the ongoing concerns of the
Aboriginal people that they would be able to play their
part in the Games. The Torch Relay was only one of the
ways in which the Sydney organisers made a massive contribution to the reconciliation process. While Freeman,
from an Aboriginal family in the northern Queensland

town of Mackay, lit the Cauldron, the first to carry the Flame when the Torch arrived from Greece in the geographical centre of Australia at Uluru – known to the rest of the world as Ayres Rock – was Nova Peris-Kneebone, a Hockey gold medallist-turned sprinter and one of 11 Aboriginal members of the team bound for Sydney. Peris-Kneebone ran with her nine-year-old daughter, Jessica, while among the 11,000 Australians to carry the Torch on its 27,000km journey around Australia was Evonne Goolagong Cawley, the Aboriginal tennis player who twice won Wimbledon.

For Australian journalists and Olympic-watchers, it was the Torch Relay that changed people's perceptions about the forthcoming Games. Jacquelin Magnay, who covered the Games for the *Sydney Morning Herald*, said: 'There were a lot of dramas for the organisers in the build up to the Games over ticket sales, the changes within the organisation and there were concerns about whether the organisation could pull this off. There was a lot of anxiety but all that changed when the Torch arrived at Uluru. There was a quantum shift in every Australian's attitude towards the Games, which went from the negative to unbridled popular support. As a journalist, you had to take note of that. Negative stories about the Games didn't wash anymore.'

As with any Olympic and Paralympic Games, the negative stories did persist, from the neighbourhoods upset that their local buses had been commandeered by the Sydney organisers, to the journalists who complained on arrival that the transportation system was inefficient or that the bed linen provided in their accommodation was not adequate against the cool nights of an Australian spring. Even this lingering negativity had all but vanished by the time Freeman lit the Cauldron, following a stunning

Opening Ceremony that had encapsulated the essence of Australia, from the 120 stockhorses and riders that began proceedings to the procession of Ned Kellys on stilts and explorers on bicycles. It was colourful, rousing, beautiful and funny, even self-mocking – and that was perhaps the Ceremony's most endearing feature. It was significant, too, that Australia's ability to laugh at itself and have fun was to be an enduring theme for the entire Olympic and Paralympic Games.

It shone through at the venues and in the attitude of the 47,000 volunteers, who went about their tasks with a smile and a sense of humour that welcomed the world to Australia's biggest party. So successful were these volunteers that they were celebrated along with the athletes after the Games and treated to a ticker-tape parade through Sydney. Many of them gathered again in September 2010 to celebrate the 10th anniversary of the Sydney 2000 Olympic and Paralympic Games.

It seemed to those lucky enough to have been at the Games that the party-like casualness of Australia's approach stemmed from the sheer exhilaration of the Opening Ceremony. Magnay added: 'The Opening Ceremony began with a strong historical reference to Aussie history and its colonial past, which went down very well. It just got better and better. People were pleasantly surprised at the sophistication of the Ceremony and the lighting. It wasn't kitsch or mundane and it ticked all the boxes. It felt like being in a largely Australian crowd so there was a great atmosphere. It was electric in the Stadium that night. It was buzzing with a sense of excitement and anticipation. It was as if this was the only time in history that the world was watching Australia and we pulled it off. The malfunction with the Cauldron, in a way, was seen as very Australian in that we're not perfect and we don't care either.

'When Sydney won the right to stage the Games in 1993, the Australian economy was struggling and the mood changed almost overnight. There followed seven years of prosperity and the Games were built on a budget that was quite healthy and a mood that was buoyant. By the end of the Ceremony, there was a feeling that it was a party to end all parties to celebrate that. It was all about showing a can-do attitude to the rest of the world and a chance to show how brilliant we were at organising events.'

Juan Antonio Samaranch, the President of the International Olympic Committee overseeing his last Games in charge, was hugely impressed by the Opening Ceremony and, two weeks later, he gave Sydney the best possible accolade. 'They could not have been better,' he said at the Closing Ceremony. 'Therefore, I am proud and happy to proclaim that you have presented to the world the best Olympic Games ever.' For Samaranch, who was forced to return to Barcelona at the beginning of the Games because of the death of his wife, Maria Therese, the Sydney 2000 Games could not have been more timely, coming as they did, in the wake of some difficult years for the IOC. It was Samaranch who steered the IOC through these and saw Sydney re-establish the Olympic Games as the greatest show on earth.

Where Atlanta 1996 was perceived as a corporate Games, Sydney duly delivered on its promise to organise an Olympic and Paralympic Games for the athletes and was the perfect Host City. The dedication to the Olympic spirit spread beyond the sporting venues and into the city itself, to the trains, hotels, harbourside restaurants and pubs. Sydney provided a template for what an Olympic Host City should be and the IOC will always be grateful to the city and to every Australian who played a part in making these a memorable Games. It is worth noting that the expertise gained in organising the Sydney event is still being used today. Australians who played significant roles then are now working in Britain to make the London 2012 Olympic and Paralympic Games the greatest ever staged. Some of those people also worked at the Games in Athens, Turin, Beijing and Vancouver; many will, no doubt, go on to add their considerable experience to the Rio de Janeiro Games in 2016.

'It was a truly wonderful day for me, and has remained so ever since'

Mary Peters, Pentathlon gold medallist in the 1972 Olympic Games.

2

AGAINST THE ODDS

Peters brings Joy to a Troubled City

Munich 1972
David Miller

Lancashire-born, Belfast raised, Mary Peters charmed the world in winning Pentathlon gold for Britain

If all three ran at their best, Mary Peters would win. In the 200m, the final event of the Pentathlon, she had to finish no more than 1.2 seconds behind the West German Heide Rosendahl and 0.8 behind Burglinde Pollak of East Germany. But this was the slender Rosendahl's specialist discipline. They lined up with Pollak in lane two, Peters in three, Rosendahl in six. Rosendahl duly ripped to the front to come home in 22.96. As her time appeared on the electronic screen, there were gasps as the crowd awaited the times for the other two. The delay seemed to take an age. It was quickly calculated that Mary needed 24.18 seconds or better. Up flashed the news: 24.08 – her third best performance of the contest. She had done it by a 10th of a second and 10 points.

'My father had been there in the crowd for the high jump, though I didn't know it at the time', Mary relates. 'He'd come from Australia where he was now living, and apparently had been busy telling all those around him that his daughter was going to win. When he went and told the BBC that he was my father, they initially didn't believe him.'

The terrorist attack on the Olympic Games in Munich was yet to unfold, but it became the sombre backdrop to Peters' triumph. In the wake of her victory, Peters had another, more personal, threat to address. On the evening following Mary's triumph, the British Olympic Association was holding a celebration party. Mary's father was there and across the room was seen to be holding an urgent conversation. What was happening, she wondered? From Lord Rupert Neville, equerry to the Duke of Edinburgh, she learned that on her return home to Belfast there were threats to her safety.

The Irish 'troubles' were intensifying. 'It was something I didn't like to talk about', Mary says. 'I didn't want to encourage a public sympathy vote back home. But at the same time, I felt slightly guilty after the tragedy the following day in the Village, not being really aware of what was happening. Janet Simpson, a colleague on the British team, said "Come and look at all these tanks around the fencing, I wonder what they're for?" We went off into town for the morning. It was only on return that we learned the news, yet were told by somebody that all the hostages had been rescued. Because of the urgency of unexpected security measures in getting me home, Munich's massacre at the time passed me by. It was a disturbing experience to think that in a different situation I could have been a victim. I loved the people at home in Belfast, and wondered whether the threat could be from someone wanting revenge, for believing that I should have been competing for Ireland instead of Britain. Yet I was born in England and could only be selected for Britain.'

Mary was accompanied home by two detectives. Her father wanted her to travel with him to Australia where he was now living, but she was intent on being back where she knew she belonged. In spite of the anxieties, there was an open-top lorry to parade her through the streets, and a welcome that was euphoric. 'I didn't go to the memorial service in Munich, I didn't even know it was taking place. I went back on the 20th anniversary of the Games in 1992, and all the emotions returned. I was reluctant to see the movie that was later released, and didn't want to comment, though I did eventually go and see it with my brother.'

Mary was born in Halewood in Lancashire in 1939, the family moving to Belfast when she was 11, her father, an insurance broker, being transferred there. When her mother died prematurely, her father remarried her mother's best friend and they and her brother emigrated to Australia. 'I had just started at college for domestic science, it was more sensible for me to stay, besides I now felt at home in Belfast. The turning point in my life was when I represented Northern Ireland in the shot-put, high jump and relay at the Commonwealth Games in Cardiff, when I was 18. Living on the Antrim Road on the north side of town, to get to the training gymnasium I needed to take two buses across town to the Queen's University track, often with bombs going off around the city. The track had potholes, and mostly I worked indoors.' Being an unsponsored amateur it was invaluable when she was awarded a Churchill Scholarship to train at Pasadena, Los Angeles, with the benefit of sunshine and relaxed travelling, plus the advantage of top-flight colleagues who could stretch her towards her full potential.

As a robust all-rounder, Mary's early excellence was

in the shot; she would compete in every Commonwealth Games from 1958 to 1974. Her first Olympic Games was the Tokyo 1964 Games where, against all expectations, she finished fourth in the Pentathlon. With the smiling modesty that marked her career, she regarded herself as little more than a companion to the glamorous Mary Rand, who was not only to take the Pentathlon silver, between Soviet amazons Irina Press and Galina Bystrova, but also to achieve gold in the Long Jump. 'I was more interested in supporting Mary, I knew she was the one with the talent, I had no thought of rising as high as fourth. Yet I loved the occasion, the feel of competition. I had so much energy I could have done six or seven events any day of the week.' She placed second in the Commonwealth Games in 1966. By the time of the Olympic Games in Mexico City two years later Mary Peters' objective, having added two stone of muscle, was as much the individual Shot as the Pentathlon. Proud captain of the team, the altitude plus a slight ankle injury undermined her performance. Arthur Gold, Honorary Secretary of the British Amateur Athletics Board, kindly wrote to say that this experience was no more than another stepping-stone.

Behind the scenes, Mary was pushed by her coach, Buster McShane, a pillar both morally and technically for a would-be champion. She also had the benefit of living in Belfast free of the media pressure placed upon other prominent athletes, such as distance runner Dave Bedford. Initially working on weight training from 1958, McShane had additionally taken over her track work in 1962, constantly advising her she had greater potential than she herself recognised. Following the Mexico City 1968 Games, McShane began metaphorically to wind the springs, never mind that violence in Belfast was escalating. If she could go to the Commonwealth Games in Edinburgh, he emphasised, and win both the Shot and Pentathlon, that would give her the confidence really to go for both at Munich 1972. Win the double in Edinburgh she did. 'I began to be convinced that I *could* win in Munich. By now I'd learned the Fosbury Flop for the high jump [an innovative style introduced by American Dick Fosbury, leaping backwards and landing on one's neck] and this had brought me an improvement of five inches [12.7cm]. The hurdles were going well, and leading up to Munich I was more concerned about Burglinde Pollak, a powerful East German who had won the European title, than I was about Heide Rosendahl, a West German who was a slim sprinter–long jumper. I'd never seen Pollak until I arrived in Munich's Village, and when I had a glimpse I felt less worried – though she was big, my impression was that she was a bit soft temperamentally.'

The first of the Pentathlon's five events (upgraded to the Heptathlon's seven in 1984) was the high hurdles. Often scheduled for the afternoon, it now began at 9.30am, in front of a full house at the then iconic new Stadium. Rosendahl won her heat in 13.34, and Pollak hers in 13.53. Mary, though second behind another East German, achieved a personal best of 13.29. This gave her a slender seven-point lead over Rosendahl, with Pollak a further three points behind.

There was a disconcerting delay prior to the shot put, Mary's strength and Rosendahl's weakest event. The three West German contenders seemed to have disappeared, and were found to be warming up on an adjacent indoor track, Marea Hartman, organiser of Britain's women's team, having to demand their return. Mary had held the British record since 1966, and in the second round now threw 16.20m, a personal best for her in the Pentathlon. With 16.04, Pollak slid further behind, Rosendahl further still and the points table now read: 1,920 Peters, 1,879 Pollak, 1,783 Rosendahl.

Rosendahl, blonde and charming, was a darling of West Germany and playing to her home crowd, yet the high jump event on this afternoon was to provide one of the highlights of the entire Games. As the progress of the event developed, the 95,000 spectators, in a mood of sporting generosity, embraced the British athlete as warmly as their own favourite. Out of character, the Belfast woman responded by blowing kisses in return, as a rivalry grew that epitomised all that is best in Olympic competition. By now, approaching evening, only the pole vault was still in action at the other end of the Stadium. 'I wasn't daunted by the crowd, I rose to them', Mary recalls. 'It was like being on stage at the theatre. Usually, the crowd never remains till the end on the first day of Pentathlon, but now they were chanting my name. They warmed to me because they could see I was enjoying the contest. It was unlike me, at that level, to respond. I should have been concentrating on jumping.'

Having entered at 1.55m, Mary recorded no failures through to 1.68m, at which height Rosendahl, using the conventional straddle style, failed. Mary twice failed at 1.71m, cleared on her third attempt, did likewise at 1.76m, Pollak failing this height. Now Mary had the Stadium to herself. Over she went at 1.78m, then 1.80m and 1.82m at first attempts, finally failing at 1.83m. This garnered 1,049 points for a total of 2,969, the biggest total ever on the first day, with Pollak 97 points down and Rosendahl adrift by 301 points in fifth place.

'Although I was well in the lead, I was not complacent

overnight', Mary says. 'Rosendahl had her best two events, the long jump and 200m, still to come, while long jump was my weakest. I really didn't think she could come back from that far, but I knew it would be close. Heide would need something near her world record in the long jump, plus a really fast 200.' Come the long jump, and Rosendahl soared to 6.84m, a centimetre short of her world record, for 1,082 points and this lifted her into third place. Mary fouled on her first jump, cleared 5.90m on her second – following a long inspection of the take-off board by the judges – and a final jump of 5.98, a distance essential for her to cling to her lead. She was now 47 points clear of Pollak and 121 ahead of Rosendahl with just the 200m to go.

'In 17 years, this was my 42nd Pentathlon, and I knew I would have to run the race of my life', Mary reflects. 'Stupidly, I'd warmed up as if I was running the first heat, whereas I would of course be in the last heat. In my anxiety and excitement I was wholly confused, and I was fortunate that this didn't make any difference. As I walked round the track to the starting line, it was wonderful to hear my name being called, to hear voices that I recognised, that people were talking about me, yet truthfully I was so scared, knowing what Heide could do, how popular she was.'

It was the race of her life. With a world record of 4,801 points, Peters became only the third woman to win an Olympic gold medal for Britain, after Mary Rand and Ann Packer (800m), both winners at the Tokyo 1964 Games. 'It was a truly wonderful day for me, and has remained so ever since,' she says. 'It cemented my affinity with Belfast, my sense of Irishness, and my years since have been a reward.'

Oscar's Triple Gold

Beijing 2008

Kevin McCallum

*70,000 people packed into the Bird's Nest to watch a
Paralympic legend win his third gold medal*

On 16 September 2008, Oscar Pistorius, lying on his bed
in the Paralympic Athletes' Village in Beijing, had a peek
outside and sighed.

It was raining. Again. It had rained just about every
day he had run at the 2008 Paralympic Games. He was
the rain man of Beijing. Back home in Pretoria all the talk
was about how the summer rains of the Gauteng province
were late that year. The sports fields of his former school,
Pretoria Boys High, were brown. The rugby fields he had
played on as a schoolboy were desperate for the down-
pours that would turn them green and lush in time for the
cricket season.

But in Beijing it rained. Later, as we flew home to South
Africa together, he would joke with me that the real reason people wanted him to come home was to bring back
with him the heavy thunderstorms the people of Gauteng
expected as a matter of course around 4pm each day.
After 30 minutes of heavy rain, thunder and lightning,
the streets of Pretoria would be washed clean, the fields
would be soaked and the summer sun would push the

clouds away for the day. In Beijing, on 16 September, at 2.57pm South African time, Pistorius was aiming to put on a 48-second show of thunder and lightning at the Bird's Nest later that evening. The 400m Final was the last track event of the Beijing 2008 Games, the showpiece scheduled thus by the organisers so they could end their programme with a bang, featuring the man who had become the most recognisable face in disability sport. For Pistorius the race would bring him his third gold medal of the Games, ending a strange year in which he had flirted with qualification to the Olympic Games and missed out.

The 400m is Pistorius's favourite event. It suits him as a double-leg amputee because it gives him enough distance to overcome the disadvantage he has at the start against the single-leg amputees. Wearing two of the Ossur Cheetah carbon fibre blades from which he takes his nickname, the Blade Runner, he has no ankle to push off against in the starting blocks. His final surge comes in the final bend, or, in the case of his 100m victory, the first of his three gold medals in Beijing, the final 30m. He had won that race by three hundredths of a second from Jerome Singleton, the American, who would become his new rival and would beat him in the 100m in the IPC World Championships in New Zealand in January 2011.

Seemingly untouchable, Pistorius needed a challenger and on a slightly damp Tuesday night in Beijing, in front of 70,000 screaming fans and after 11.17 seconds of sprinting, Pistorius found the adversary with whom he will duel for the title of fastest disabled athlete in the world for as long as the two compete. Singleton pushed Pistorius to run the fastest 60m of his career to beat him to the 100m gold medal in Beijing. Pistorius admitted then he would be watching Singleton carefully, which echoed what another

American, Marlon Shirley, said when he beat Pistorius in the 100m in Athens but lost to him in the 200m.

The similarities between Pistorius and Singleton are spooky. Pistorius was born without fibulas and had his legs amputated halfway between his knees and ankles as an 11-month-old infant; Singleton was born without the fibula in his right leg and had his lower leg removed as a child; they both learned to walk with prosthetics from a young age and walk without a limp; they both took up competitive running late in life; Pistorius played rugby at school; Singleton played American Football; and they were born just six months apart.

The 100m was the most dramatic of all Pistorius's three events. The 200m a few days after was won with relative ease in 21.67secs, almost a second ahead of Jim Bob Bizzell from the United States, with Briton Ian Jones in third. The 100m was a different beast. Starting in lane five, Pistorius had Shirley on his left-hand side and Singleton on his right. Two lanes to his left was Brian Frasure, who had balanced Pistorius's first set of blades before the Athens 2004 Games. It was to be his last Paralympic Games before he retired from competition. A lane further down from Frasure was Arnu Fourie, the single-leg amputee South African. Pistorius, usually one to joke and smile before a race, was more nervous than usual. Sitting on the block, his tracksuit top off, he looked around, caught the eye of a friend and gave a quick smile. His pre-race warm-up had changed somewhat from Athens. In Greece he would take a bottle of ice-cold water and pour it on himself to 'make me wake up a bit'. In Beijing the expectations of the world meant he was as awake as he will ever be.

Shirley had the hood of his jacket up and looked

straight ahead. He had been talking big ahead of the Games, talking himself up and Pistorius down. Yet he had avoided running against Pistorius in competition in the build-up to the Games, which prompted the South African to wonder aloud if he was more talk than walk. It was not the IAAF who first complained that Pistorius was getting an advantage from his prosthetic Cheetah limbs, but Shirley. 'He's able to manipulate something that's out of other athletes' control,' Shirley told *Sports Illustrated*. 'Just because he has a double amputation, why should he have a different set of rules?' It was a weird accusation from Shirley, who was also sponsored by Ossur, the Finland-based company that make Cheetah prosthetics. Pistorius had spooked Shirley and it showed.

Then the race. Bang. They were off. Mostly. Pistorius had a horrid start, worse than usual. Singleton and Shirley got off to a flyer, the former leading with Pistorius almost 6m adrift. Fourie told me later that at about halfway he was wondering where his Paralympic Village roommate was. A second later he found out as Pistorius blasted past him just after the 50m mark. Shirley's hamstring went and he fell hard, almost taking out Frasure. Singleton looked to have the win locked up, but as he edged towards the line, Pistorius never eased his stride, hit top speed, dipped his head on the line and snatched the gold.

'Yes, I did think I had won that,' said Singleton, who did not know he had been pipped on the line until he looked up at the big screen. 'I knew that if I saw Oscar the race was over. At the end I didn't think I saw him, but he dipped on me and took me on the line. I'm just happy to be here with all these great athletes. Oscar is the best and I want to race against the best.'

For Pistorius it was the closest he had come to failing

since 2004, when he had fallen out of the blocks in the 200m semi-final in Athens, and, in his own words 'caught the biggest fright of my life'. In that race he had to come from behind and flew down the final 60m to win.

'When you have a bad start like I did and you look up and you're 6m or 7m behind everyone already, you know that you are in for a hard race,' said Pistorius. 'The wet was not good for sprinting because you are putting that much more power down on the track. So, you're worried about slipping in the first couple of metres because you are putting more power down before you get into your stride. Mentally it puts you back a bit because you know you're going to be slipping. We're only allowed 7mm spikes, but I always run with the maximum.'

Pistorius attracted maximum crowds and attention in Beijing. He has done so ever since he burst on to the scene at the Athens 2004 Games. The word for 'fast' in Mandarin is *kuai*; the word for 'foot' is *jiao*. Put them together and you get 'Oscar Pistorius', except the Blade Runner is pretty *kuai* without any *jiao*. Pistorius is a highly talented athlete who just happens to have been born a little differently to two parents who took the brave and hard decision to amputate the lower limbs of their 11-month-old baby. They could have opted for a series of operations that might have allowed him to walk with a severe limp, but Henke and the late Sheila Pistorius, who died when Pistorius was 15 and remains his motivation for running, met with other amputee children and saw a future for their boy.

They consulted several orthopaedic surgeons to find out the best doctors to perform the amputation and discovered that one of the top three in the world, Gerry Versveld, was in South Africa. He removed Pistorius's legs in a three-hour operation. Almost 17 years later Versveld was in the stands in Athens as Pistorius won gold. Six months after the operation Pistorius was walking on stumps, already independent. He was bullied in primary school, but after being pushed over by one boy, grabbed him and kicked him on the chin with his prosthetic limb. The bullying stopped.

He hated athletics and admitted that he would forge sick notes to get out of cross-country runs at school. Instead he played water polo, rugby and tennis at Pretoria Boys High and jokes that there were times when one of his artificial legs would come off during a match, which would be a little disconcerting for the boys he played against. Legend tells of how he walked out to bat in a cricket game without pads: 'leg before' decisions took on a new meaning. It was rugby that prompted him to start his athletics career after a knee injury forced him to go for rehabilitation at the University of Pretoria. Six months after that injury he was racing at Athens in the Paralympic Games. He became a star then, the teenage boy became a man and the world fell in love with him.

He dominated the world of Paralympic sprinting after Athens, but had ambitions to run at the Olympic Games. His fellow South African, Natalie du Toit, the single-leg amputee who lost a limb when a car crashed into her in Cape Town, qualified for the Open Water Marathon at the Beijing 2008 Olympic Games. Pistorius found the IAAF initially welcoming, inviting him to compete in meets, but when it looked like he wanted more, they launched an investigation into whether his carbon fibre limbs gave him an advantage. Pistorius was subjected to a series of tests and then subsequently banned by the IAAF from able-bodied sport. They did not expect the public backlash that followed, nor the fact that one of the top law firms in the world, Dewey & LeBoeuf, would take his case on *pro bono* and represented him at the Court of Arbitration for Sport. They won, and Pistorius's dream of being allowed to qualify for the Olympic Games continued. Yet the case had taken up so much of his time that he had lost three months of training. An intense period of training with coach Ampie Louw followed, during which he dropped his body weight and came into the Beijing 2008 Paralympic Games as ready as he could be. The Olympic Games would have to wait.

'Running in the Olympics would be amazing but in many ways the Paralympics are even more special. Why? The passion the athletes have for their sport is unbelievable. The cerebral palsy runners know their condition can't get any better, but I defy anyone to watch them and not see them as fully dedicated athletes who train as hard as any Olympian. Before I was exposed to the Paralympics, like most people I thought they were second best in some way. How wrong can you be? In the Olympics of 2016, I firmly believe each and every finalist in each and every Paralympic event will have an Olympic qualifying time,' said Pistorius.

On 16 September 2008 Pistorius walked out on to the track at the Bird's Nest as a proud Paralympian. He was not feeling well, a cold he had picked up just before the 200m Final could not be shaken. The track was wet after the heavens had opened and drenched it – but then again that was nothing new for him at these Games. Besides, there are people who think Pistorius walks on water. The rain certainly did not deter a capacity crowd. The day before I had sent him a text message suggesting that he might want to ask his new sponsor, Pirelli, the Italian tyre manufacturer, for a set of wet weather rubber for his blades. He laughed, then said he had a point to prove. 'The 400m is the race I have been putting all my time and energy and training into. Everything has been focused towards it and I'm hoping I'll show that.'

He was in lane four this time. I was sitting in the press benches on the finish line as they announced his name and the roar of approval rolled around like the thunder had done a few hours before. Next to me a colleague, an older journalist from South Africa, had fallen asleep in his chair. I nudged him awake and suggested he might not want to miss this.

The only question the commentators had about the athlete with number 1918 pinned to his vest was 'how fast will he go?' Fast. His start was steady, but as he took the small steps he and Louw had worked on to speed up his early momentum he was soon up to third and then second as they hit the final bend, flying past the discus cage on the inside of the track. The Bird's Nest erupted as the Blade Runner, in the calm of the storm that rolled across the Chinese capital, flew down the final straight to break the world record and confirm he was the fastest man on no legs.

The win was, like every one of his victories, for his mother. Her birthday is tattooed on the inside of his right bicep. When he was just 17 months old his mother had written him a letter, the words of which have defined his life. 'Feet cannot earn a good salary or give us a compassionate and loving heart. A loser is not the one who runs last in the race. It is the one who sits and watches and has never tried to run.'

First Tango in Paris ...

Paris 1924
Doug Gillon

'I run the first 200 as hard as I can ... then, for the second 200, with God's help, I run harder.'
Eric Liddell, athlete and missionary

Eric Liddell stands, hands on hips, accepts a congratulatory handshake from the runner-up, and permits himself a gentle smile. There is no hint of distress. Indeed, he does not even seem out of breath. How can this be? He has just won Olympic gold over 400m at the Paris 1924 Games. Despite running without view of the opposition (due to the stagger) in the outside lane of six, he has destroyed a field that includes two men who had beaten the Olympic Games record in earlier rounds.

He had never raced the distance before lining up for the heats. Indeed, when 1924 dawned, Liddell's ambitions lay at 100m. Yet he had broken the mould for 400m. Sprinting flat out from the gun, he prompted the cognoscenti to wonder how soon he would 'blow up'. Instead, head back, Liddell drew further clear as the white worsted of the finishing line approached. Joseph Imbach, the Swiss who had set a new record in his heat, pulled up, while J. Coard Taylor (winner of the US Olympic Trial) fell close to the line. To confirm it all, the man in the straw boater held the wind gauge aloft and pronounced that Liddell's time of 47.6 seconds was a world record. His winning margin over American Horatio Fitch was four fifths of a second in the jargon of the day. It took 72 years before there was a wider one.

Colombes Stadium was familiar to Liddell. Two years earlier, when he was still just 19, he had played rugby here on the left wing for his country and had been narrowly denied a try as Scotland drew with France. The track measured 500m, with one bend and two straights. Some of the crowd hung over the fence, watching the runners excavate their holes. This was the era before starting blocks, and Liddell, who had a sportsman's reputation for sharing his trowel, walked back to shake the hand of each rival.

He had plenty of time. Punctilious modern scheduling had yet to be imposed, and when the pipe major suggested to the band of the second battalion, the Queen's Own Cameron Highlanders, 'Let's gie the lad a blaw', they responded with alacrity, and French officials could do nothing to silence the nerve-tingling encouragement. The pipes skirled the stirring battle tune 'The Campbells are Coming' and the kilts picked up their habitual momentum, swinging in time to the march of the drummers. Earlier Liddell had been in a group that followed the band up the Champs-Elysées, to lay a wreath on the tomb of the Unknown Warrior. This had been a poignant moment given how many Olympians had fallen in the Great War, among them the only Scot then to have won Athletics gold, Wyndham Halswelle – in the very event that Liddell was about to win.

The national flags that billowed in a strong crosswind on 11 July heralded the arrival of a man ahead of his time: Liddell, defying custom and convention in the name of God. Two days earlier he had won bronze in the 200m. It would be Atlanta 1996 before Michael Johnson became the next claimant to medals in both the 200m and the 400m.

Records come and go. Liddell's 400m time survived as a European and British best until 1936, while his world mark was written out in 1926. The international federation ruled that Ted Meredith's time for 440 yards (slightly further) was superior. However, Liddell had won immortality, inspiring the film *Chariots of Fire*. The script strayed from the facts, but the key moments were all true. Liddell really was uplifted by a note passed to him before the race in the Hotel Moderne, for example. Paraphrasing 1 Samuel 2:30, it had come from one of the team masseurs, and read 'In the old book it says: "He that honours me I will honour". Wishing you the best of success always.' The author was not a screenplay rival, but the note was fact.

Celluloid mythology played a part, of course. Liddell actually learned programme details in January and saw that the opening round of the short sprint (at which he held the British record) was on a Sunday. Citing his Sabbatarian principles, he withdrew. Attempts to persuade him that the continental Sabbath ended at midday were dismissed. 'My Sunday lasts all day', he told athletics historian David Jamieson. Instead, he opted for the 400m six months before the Games, preparing accordingly. Liddell's decision to uphold his principles was castigated in the domestic press, which reported an implicit rebuke from Lord Cadogan. Liddell remained resolute, but many years later he revealed to his wife, Florence, that he'd been profoundly hurt. 'He was called a traitor to his country, and I think he felt it quite keenly,' she said.

The British Olympic Association tried in vain to amend the Paris programme, and Harold Abrahams, co-hero of *Chariots of Fire*, won the 100m. Yet he came nowhere near the double. When Liddell took 200m bronze, Abrahams was last. Liddell had beaten him in the 100 yards at the Amateur Athletic Association Championships the previous year. Liddell's time of 9.7 was just a tenth outside the world record, and survived for 35 years as the UK best, until 1958 when it was lowered by Peter Radford, the bronze medallist at the Rome 1960 Games. Abrahams pleaded a throat infection for that defeat, although he did break the British record to win the Long Jump title.

Speculation as to what might have happened had the 100m heats not been on the Sabbath is fruitless. However, Liddell would clearly have been selected for both relays had they not also been on Sunday. Britain took silver in the 4x100m behind the US, and came third in the 4x400m. Just a week after Paris, Liddell joined three of that Olympic bronze-medal quartet and anchored the British Empire to victory over the US Olympic champions in a 4x440 yard relay. He retrieved a seven-yard deficit on Olympic silver medallist Fitch, and won by four.

Two additional medals from relays would have given Liddell a haul of four from those Olympic Games. Not that he saw the medals he did win for ages. There were no Victory Ceremonies, and they arrived by post at his Edinburgh home months later.

By way of celebration after his 400m victory, Liddell joined Arthur Marshall, a member of the GB Relay squad. According to Marshall, he and Liddell went off to enjoy a tango in Paris with two American girls. Legend has it that Liddell hurried back to his hotel, to the room he shared with 800m champion Douglas Lowe. He had a sermon to prepare for the following day at the Scots Kirk in Paris. Liddell did indeed preach there the next day, but not before he and Marshall had spent part of the evening at a Tango Tea Dance on the Champs-Elysées.

Marshall, who was later knighted and lived to the age of 100, told how they had struck up an acquaintance with sisters Freddie and Edith on board *The Republic*, during the 10-day boat trip back from the Pennsylvania Relays. They had all arranged to meet in Paris while the pair were 'doing Europe', and Marshall described how Liddell had donned fancy dress and played cards on the voyage, confounding perceptions of the Scot – a noted temperance campaigner – as a stuffed shirt and kill joy.

Yet compelling aspects of Liddell's story have been almost air brushed from history. Edinburgh's Waverley Station was mobbed on his return, and six days after his Olympic Games victory he graduated as a BSc at Edinburgh University where the principal joked: 'You have shown that none can pass you but the examiner'. Afterwards he was chaired shoulder high through the streets, with an oleaster wreath on his head. It had been provided by the Royal Botanical Gardens – the closest they had to olive.

Liddell was doted on with a fervour likened to the Beatle-mania of the 1960s. Women liked his muscular Christianity, and young men reportedly packed churches, squeezing onto pulpit steps to hear him preach. He spent a year at Divinity College, also turning his back on rugby in a year in which Scotland won a rare Grand Slam. He had scored 10 tries in two trials for Scotland and played in seven internationals, losing only once. After college, in 1925, he followed his father and brother, Rob, to work for the London Missionary Society in China. When he left Edinburgh, the station was packed. An eyewitness reported Liddell himself starting to sing, hymn 388, 'Jesus shall reign where'er the sun...' It was taken up throughout the station and tears flowed as the train pulled out.

He travelled by the Trans-Siberian Railway to Tientsin, Northern China. There he raised funds for a track modelled on Stamford Bridge, where he had won the AAA title. It was considered one of the finest tracks in Asia, yet this was only a small part of a great legacy.

Liddell remained an athlete. In 1928 he beat French and Japanese Olympians over 200m and 400m at the South Manchurian Railway celebrations in China. He also raced Dr Otto Peltzer, the German world 800m and 1,500m record holder. He beat Peltzer at 400m, and narrowly lost at 800m. Peltzer urged him to go for the 800m at the Los Angeles 1932 Games, saying, 'If he trained, he could be the greatest man in the world at that distance.'

When Britons were interned in Japan after the Sino-Japanese war, Liddell was among them. And so there was a captive audience for his final race, far removed from the cheers of Colombes. In that Japanese internment camp in Shandong Province, the young David Michell was an eyewitness to a handicap for veterans, 'middle-aged runners, weakened by the rigours and poor food of camp life.' By then in his early 40s, Liddell was back-marker, yet he won.

Liddell had sent his pregnant wife and two daughters to safety in Canada in 1941, and he became a teacher and surrogate father to many children in the camp. Michell, who went on to become a minister, wrote a book on his childhood. He recalled how Liddell mixed glue from fish bladders and scales to mend hockey sticks, working by night to spare inmates the smell. The man who had declined to run the 100m at the Olympic Games on the Sabbath refereed hockey on Sundays to stop young-sters fighting. He would cannibalise scraps of curtains and sheets to make baseballs. Liddell also turned down a chance of repatriation, giving his place instead to an expectant mother. When British Olympic Association per-formance director Sir Clive Woodward laid a wreath on Liddell's grave, Chinese officials volunteered the infor-mation that Sir Winston Churchill had also tried to broker his release.

Liddell died in February 1945, of a brain tumour. The children he had nurtured were the cord-bearers when he was buried in the snows of northern China. His grave was marked by a wooden cross, with his name in shoe polish. Its whereabouts lay unknown for 45 years. Near the spot there is now a 2m-high stone of Mull granite. Yet Liddell's body is not there. It was moved to the Mausoleum of Martyrs, some 250km southwest of Beijing, the last rest-ing place of those who gave their lives for the liberation of China. Liddell is one of a few foreigners (and fewer Christians) accorded the privilege. Though intriguingly I met Chinese during the Beijing 2008 Games who referred to him as their first Olympic champion; he was born in Tianjin, where his parents were missionaries. The most recent of many books on Liddell, *Running the Race* by John Keddie, was published in Mandarin in 2008, going on to sell more copies in China than in Britain.

Liddell's hand has reached down the years to inspire two other Scottish-born Olympic champions. When Allan Wells became Britain's first Olympic 100m winner since Abrahams, at Moscow in 1980, he was asked, 'Were you thinking of Harold Abrahams when you crossed the line, Allan?' 'No,' he replied, 'I was thinking of Eric Liddell, actually.' Wells was Scotland's first Olympic Athletics champion since 1924 – and he knew it.

Fast-forward 20 years to Sydney 2000. Ayrshire-born Stephanie Cook had been given Sally Magnusson's Liddell biography, *The Flying Scotsman*, while a cross-country runner at Oxford. It was inscribed 'to the Flying Scotswoman'. Cook ran from eighth to first in the final discipline to win the inaugural women's Olympic Modern Pentathlon title. A year later she added the world title, and retired on the spot. Two days later Dr Cook flew to ravaged Gujarat with Merlin, the medical charity. She told me Liddell had become her inspiration. Like him, she chose a life of service.

Yet for all his talent, Liddell could never beat the Scottish 440 yards record. This was held from 1906 until 1958 by Wyndham Halswelle, the London 1908 Olympic 400m champion. Liddell and Halswelle remain Britain's only Olympic 400m champions, and both were victims of war. Cut down by a single shot from a German sniper in the trenches at Neuve Chappelle, Halswelle was buried in a hastily dug grave. He was 32. A contemporary sketch in his family's possession shows a simple wooden cross, eerily similar to that of Liddell 30 years later. Eventually Halswelle's remains, like those of Liddell, were re-interred, in a military cemetery near Armentières. His gravestone makes no mention of his Olympic Games feats.

Five Star Gold

Sydney 2000
Nick Townsend

Too close for comfort, but no rival and no illness could stop Steve Redgrave from winning a fifth gold medal

At the start the atmosphere was quiet, subdued – just a couple of photographers lurking and television cameramen training their lenses. But Steve Redgrave knew that a near-capacity 24,000 spectators were lined along the course, many parading union flags. It was vital that he didn't get caught up in the British supporters' fever of anticipation.

There it was, hanging tantalisingly, like the shiniest apple in the orchard, just out of his grasp: a prize that would transform him from a phenomenon into a superman. Not his description, but that of a British media who would have helped to tow him over the line. But the 38-year-old from Marlow, who had first sat in a rowing boat as a big-framed 1.95m schoolboy because he fancied 'a good skive' nearly a quarter of a century earlier, knew it was crucial to block out all thoughts of victory. In the preceding days, he had told himself this repeatedly, 'Don't get carried away with all this hype, Steve.'

He had recalled what people had said to him in the preceding months. The father of one of the New Zealand crew that had performed a rare feat and beaten the GB Four at a regatta in Lucerne had waved Redgrave over afterwards and said, 'I really want you to win in Sydney, but the trouble is you're racing my son.' He had found that 'really weird'. Yet it confirmed to him that, in other people's eyes, he was doing something extraordinary.

Now he existed in his own world: a kingdom of four. The hulking figure of Matthew Pinsent in the stroke seat, the blond-haired Tim Foster just ahead of him and the brooding James Cracknell behind. There could be political upheaval at home, pestilence, flood and drought elsewhere, but right at that moment their endeavours were the only thing that mattered. Even family were out of mind.

Hell, he had reflected more than once in his career, had no fury like the build-up to a final of an Olympic Games. It was not the physical pain, the lactic acid piling up within his body until it felt like 'a seizure', as he described it. It was the waiting, the hanging around before the start light turned green. That was the mental torment that had gripped his entire being before every one of his previous four Olympic Finals. That is what happens when the accumulation of four years of preparation to perform is all justified, or not, by one race lasting a mere six minutes. For an Olympian, you get one chance, every four years. It's a desperately long wait for atonement.

Yet, strangely, this race, on Saturday 3 September 2000, a race that Redgrave knew would be the finale to his illustrious career, was different. Four years previously, before the final at Atlanta 1996, he had felt 'controlled panic'. As he prepared himself for the Fours final at the start line on Penrith Lakes in Sydney there was, like the 2,000m of water that stretched behind him, almost a calmness. A kind of inner peace, and, yes, of expectation.

The build-up to Sydney had been punctuated by self-doubt about his ability to stay the course. Yet now he felt good. It felt unreal, he was to explain later. He was almost enjoying the moment too much as he prepared for those 360 seconds that could, indeed should – because Team GB had assembled the best crew – bring him an unprecedented fifth Olympic gold medal.

Yet, for many of us who had followed Redgrave's career, and particularly the four years preceding Sydney, the wonder was that he and his three fellow crew members – Pinsent, Cracknell and Foster – were here, and intact. From the outside, there had been a whole litany of reasons to be uneasy. The GB Four had been the equivalent of a beautifully constructed classic car spluttering and misfiring; anything but a smooth runner.

There had been emotional strain for Cracknell. Foster's long-term back problem, a lumbar-spine strain, had been compounded by a severing of tendons when he jerked his hand back extravagantly at a Boat Race party in Oxford in 1998 and thrust it through a window pane. For anyone else it would have been excruciating and inconvenient. For one of the nation's Sydney-bound oarsmen it was close to criminal. 'Have I blown everything, not just for me, but for three others?' Foster had thought. Fortunately, he pulled through on both counts.

But the gravest worries concerned Redgrave who, in his own words, had undergone 'frustration, worry and pain' in those four preceding years. Having been diagnosed with ulcerative colitis in 1992, the oarsman discovered in late 1997 that he had Type 1 diabetes. The average, sedentary man can continue to live a near ordinary life. It is entirely different for an elite sportsman undertaking a power-based activity because of the dietary demands and the need to control sugar levels. For a time, it threatened his Olympic Games ambitions. Yet, though he never considered spurning the sport to which he had dedicated his life, Redgrave's descent into despair was such that he conceded, at one time, the possibility of 'it quitting me'.

On top of all that, the Four had arrived in Sydney having been defeated in the last regatta of the season, at Lucerne. They finished fourth, and Pinsent was to declare later 'the other crews smelled trouble like a bad cologne'. It was attributed to 'over-training' and a one-off. But questions had been asked. Could there be an anticlimactic end to Redgrave's quest for a final Olympic Games triumph?

Redgrave always placed such a reverse in perspective. He insisted that few crews, or athletes in other sports, emerge from such a four-year period without having suffered any setbacks. 'You live with it, deal with it and get on with it — as long as you're convinced when you get to that final race that you're quicker and better than anyone else,' he once told me.

An hour before the Sydney 2000 Fours Final, the GB Pairs, Ed Coode and Greg Searle, had set out from this same start in pursuit of a medal. Would their performance prove portentous? There had been a time when Coode, substitute for Foster in the Fours when it secured gold in the 1999 World Championships, may have forced his way into the Fours crew when Redgrave's state of health was affecting training performances. He had become inconsistent and there were bouts of self-doubt. There was also a subtle shift of the power-base. At the Olympic Games of Los Angeles 1984 (in the Fours), of Seoul 1988 (in the Pairs, with Andy Holmes), and of Barcelona 1992 (with Pinsent), he had been the strongest component. By the Atlanta 1996 Games, Pinsent started matching him. Redgrave, for so long the Herculean figure of British rowing, hadn't found it easy to cope with 'no longer being performing top dog'.

Redgrave insists, however, that though he always felt he could perform at the 'gold standard' there was an instant when he could have stepped down. 'For all your passion and desire, you can't kid yourself,' he said once. 'One of my strongest traits is realism.' It had been his hardest decision to go to GB head coach Jürgen Gröbler's room in April and say 'You've got to put Ed in with Matt', initially for early season trials in which the crew rowed in Pairs. He was aware, however, that if the strategy had been successful there would probably have been no way back for him. Yet, though Gröbler had stressed that no-one's seat was safe – not even Redgrave's – the coach was aware that the talisman brought other crucial qualities to the crew: notably experience and mental strength. 'That's rubbish,' Gröbler had retorted. 'Why are you putting yourself down? There's no reason for it.' Coode had accepted the decision phlegmatically and a medal of some hue had been anticipated from his powerful new partnership with Searle.

The Four had actually changed their routine because Gröbler had wanted to watch the Pairs. Normally Redgrave would meet the others at the boat an hour before the start to go through their race tactics one final time and then go for a warm-up run. This time they switched the schedule, went for a run first down the side of the lake and watched the Pairs come down. In the end they finished a frustrating fourth, after appearing to be set for a medal. It was as disappointing for the British team as the triumph of the Eights the following morning would be a source of euphoria. There is a Loctite bond between members of different GB crews, with vicarious delight at success, and profound disappointment at defeat.

Redgrave couldn't afford to dwell on the Pair's misfortune. All that went through his mind – just a passing thought, he stresses, however – is that having won the Pairs, with Pinsent in Los Angeles 1984, that suddenly he was no longer a reigning Olympic champion. There were 50 minutes before he could re-establish that status, albeit in a different boat.

His entire focus now was on ensuring that the Four displayed no vulnerability. The role of 'senior man' brought with it responsibility. Foster had rowed at the previous Games, gaining a bronze in the Fours at Atlanta 1996. Cracknell was a three-time World Champion but had not competed before at an Olympic Games. Now, they had one huge advantage: rowing with two men boasting tremendous Olympic success. Redgrave was entirely confident the less experienced pair could 'hold it together'. However, Cracknell had been nervous and twitchy at times, according to Redgrave. 'It's alright, James,' he had told Cracknell, who had been seemingly close to tears in the hour before the start. 'We're going to win this. No problem.'

That attitude exemplified the man. Pinsent knew that there was one guarantee: the Games environment always galvanised Redgrave, for whom the old adage 'the bigger the event, the better I perform' invariably applied. And Redgrave himself knew the Four were back on form. The heat and semi-final had demonstrated that. But also the highly rational oarsman knew that, for all their highly publicised problems, they'd only lost twice in four years. At any level of sport, that is an outstanding record.

There was too an inescapable logic in Redgrave's race plan. Other crews might like to take it steady over the first half of the 2000m race, conserving their energies for a strong finish. Redgrave had never favoured such tactics. With Pinsent in the pair and now again in the Four, he – and Grobler – preferred to keep it simple. If you're the strongest and fastest crew in the race, do not complicate things: get out in front and stay there. The plan made the most of the British Four's strengths and challenged the mental toughness of the other crews. The idea of rowing through a Four with Redgrave and Pinsent on board was a massive psychological hurdle for every oarsman who had spent years following in the British pair's wash. Just because this was the most important race of Redgrave's life was no reason for the British Four to change their habits.

In lane three of six finalists, the GB Four surged ahead of their rivals, Italy, the USA, New Zealand, Australia and Slovenia, in a mere eight lengths and were comfortably fastest over the first 500m. Italy were quickest over the next 500m. But it was GB who set the pace again over the third quarter. Although the British crew were only fourth fastest in the last 500m, Redgrave, making the calls, knew that there was never a stage when Italy, who finished runners-up by 0.38 of a second, or any other crew would row through them. As the line of bubbles under the water, indicating the finish, approached, the GB men eased down.

It hurt, badly. Redgrave knew it would … for maybe 5, 10, 15 minutes. But he reminded himself, 'I'm going to be five-times Olympic champion for the rest of my life.' It was only later, scrutinising the video that Redgrave exclaimed, 'S**t, that's quite close!' He has always denied, though, that the gold was ever in jeopardy. 'It's all about judgement, and we got it right,' he has said insouciantly.

At the press conference afterwards, he was given a standing ovation. Normally cynical journalists asked him to sign their Olympic Games accreditation passes – a gesture that genuinely took him aback. It had simply been a job well done. What the Four had set out and trained and prepared to do, with some interruptions along the way, had come to fruition.

His last day at the office was over. For an elite sportsman it's no cause for a party. 'In sport your last day at the office is usually the most important', as Redgrave put it. Yet, those six minutes – 5 min 56.24, to be precise – at Sydney transformed his life for ever. A knighthood followed and a public recognition that transcended sport. Even all these years on, people remember the time, the day, the place when an essentially shy, modest man, blessed with a prodigious talent, became Britain's greatest Olympian.

'We had a quiet confidence about our form and what we could do, and if we did those things we were really, really confident that we could win the gold medal'

Troy Sachs, Paralympic Basketball legend.

3
GREAT TEAM EFFORTS

The Greatest Team Ever?

Helsinki 1952

David Miller

How the Magical Magyars began a football revolution

In the 1950s Mátyás Rákosi, who described himself as 'Stalin's best pupil' and who ran the satellite communist state of Hungary, put in motion a process that would lead to the formation of arguably the most elegant football team the world has ever seen – not excluding those wonderful Brazilians of the 1970 FIFA World Cup. The Magical Magyars were, in their prime, a coordinated spectacle that bewildered opposition and mesmerised spectators. Their fame reached its pinnacle one night at Wembley Stadium in 1953, but they first came to notice internationally as champions at the Helsinki 1952 Games on a golden day for Hungary.

The Football tournament at the Olympic Games in Helsinki witnessed a mass entry from Soviet bloc nations, six of them drawn in the preliminary round from which Scandinavia and other countries were exempted. The Soviet Union disposed of Bulgaria 2-1, all goals in extra time, while Hungary, undefeated since May 1950, beat Romania by the same score. In the first round proper the Soviet Union, taken to a 5-5 draw after extra time by an exceptional Yugoslavia side (Bobrov, the Soviet captain, scoring three times in the second half after Yugoslavia led 4-0), then lost 3-1 in the replay. Such was the perceived disgrace that the result was not officially reported nor mentioned back home in Moscow until after Stalin's death the following year. Meanwhile Hungary trounced Italy 3-0, and fully blossomed in putting seven goals past Turkey in the quarter-final and six past Sweden in the semi-final. In the latter game, Ferenc Puskás struck in the first minute, while Sándor Kocsis and Nándor Hidegkuti between them hit three goals in an amazing four minutes in the second half. The stage was set for a politically charged final between Yugoslavia and Hungary.

Behind the rise of the Hungarian side lay the organisational hand of Mátyás Rákosi. Born in the village of Ada in 1892, in the then Austro-Hungarian Empire, now Vojvodina in Serbia, Rákosi repudiated Judaism and served in the army during the First World War. He was captured, but on returning to Hungary joined the communist government, fleeing to the Soviet Union when the government fell. Returning again to Hungary in 1924 he was imprisoned, only to be released back to the Soviet Union in 1940, in exchange for Hungarian revolutionary banners from the First World War. He was finally despatched back to Hungary once more in January 1945 to organise a new Communist Party and, under Stalin's direction, the nationalisation of sport.

A Hungarian talent for ball games and gymnastics had long been evident. Arthur Rowe, later renowned as manager of Spurs, discovered Hungarian skills when coaching there before the war. Kispest, a leading club founded in 1908, had supplied players for the national team for the second FIFA World Cup in 1934, as well as Ferenc Puskás, father of the player who would become an international legend. As General Secretary of the Communist Party, one of Rákosi's first appointments was for Mihály Farkas, Minister of Defence, to take charge of sport under nationalisation. The political regime was a brutal one, with over an estimated 350,000 administrators, intellectuals and perceived opponents being purged over 10 years up to the Revolution of 1956. An early move by Farkas was to merge the Kispest club with Honvéd, the army team under control of foremost coach Gusztáv Sebes. Already with Kispest were Puskás junior and József Bozsik, each to become among the most illustrious players in history. Under nationalisation, three more budding stars were transferred from Ferencváros FC – Sándor Kocsis, Zoltán Czibor and László Budai. Further transfers were goalkeeper Gyula Grosics, centre back Gyula Lóránt, plus left back Mihály Lantos and Nándor Hidegkuti, the last player a phenomenon in midfield from MTK police club – subsequently taken over by AVH's secret police. Here was assembled a veritable academy of football geniuses.

Puskás and Bozsik made their debut for Kispest in 1943, the club at that time coached by Béla Guttman, one of Europe's leading football brains. Role models for Puskás and Bozsik as boys were England and Arsenal renowned centre forwards Ted Drake and Charlie Buchan. Bozsik's creative skills in midfield would pave the way for relentless attacking by Honvéd and the national team. While the majority of Honvéd players held nominal army rank – Puskás ultimately promoted to Major – Bozsik was a deputy in parliament, though it was alleged he was never heard to speak. Puskás by the age of 16 was already an evident genius, able to juggle not just a football but a tennis ball on instep and thigh, as though it were an additional limb. Hidegkuti had perfected his

touch in street football, developing tactical vision com-
parable to Paul Gascoigne. The mechanics were in place
for something truly spectacular: this was not just the first
flowering of a brilliant generation of players from an
unknown, oppressed nation, but also the introduction of
a new footballing ideology. Before Johan Cruyff and the
Dutch expression of 'Total Football' came Ferenc Puskás
and the Magical Magyars.

Nowadays, the numbers on players' shirts can bear little relation to their positional play. Sixty years ago, full-
backs were numbers 2 and 3, the half-back line was 4,
5 and 6, the wingers were 7 and 11, inside forwards
were 8 and 10, and the centre forward was number 9.
Formations then were predominantly what was termed
WM: that is, three defenders (full-backs and centre half),
four midfielders (wing halves and inside forwards) and
three attackers (wingers and centre forward). It was common for one of the inside forwards to be a striker alongside the centre forward, thus creating a 3–3–4 formation.
In fact, Hungary formed the outlines of what was known
as 'Total Football' as personified by Holland and then
Germany, with effectively all players attackers when in
possession, all defenders when the opposition had the
ball. Though Lóránt was a basically defensive centre half,
their formation was 3–3–4. Budai and Czibor were on the
wings, Kocsis and Puskás the central strikers. Hidegkuti,
though wearing number 9, played deep as creator alongside Bozsik and József Zakariás.

The final against Yugoslavia, who had eliminated
Germany, was shot through with political tension.
Amalgamated Balkan nations ruled by Marshall Tito,
dissenter from the Soviet bloc, were so politically 'incor-
rect' that the government in Budapest only approved a

live radio broadcast from Finland on the morning of the match. There was no television coverage. For millions of suppressed Hungarians, however, their football team's fortune was their most precious public identity. The final, on 2 August 1952, the penultimate day of the Games, was an immeasurable emotional climax. With three gold medals already achieved on that last day for a total of 15 – by László Papp in Light Welter Weight Boxing, in Water Polo and by their women's Swimming Freestyle Relay quartet – Football had the country riveted beside their radios.

A Hungarian proverb says that if the last step of a journey is successful, the rest of your life will be happy. Thus it was agony when Puskás missed a penalty, awarded by the English referee Arthur Ellis in the first half. Anxiety continued, for here against them was the kernel of a Yugoslav team that would be formidable throughout the next decade, with players such as Vladimir Beara in goal, Branko Stankovic, one of the best left-backs ever, and constant fireworks from the likes of Zlatko Cajkovski, Vujadin Boskov, Bernard Vukas and Stjepan Bobek. Puskás, however, made amends by giving Hungary the lead in the 70th minute, and Czibor ensured gold two minutes from time. A crowd of almost 60,000 witnessed the Hungarians' triumph, but few direct accounts of the game remain. Its significance to the international game only became apparent the following year at Wembley.

Back home, the public celebrated for a week. Each player was rewarded with a new car – never mind that an East German Wartburg was alarmingly prone to premature old age – and could be sure of an otherwise enhanced lifestyle in a country piteously without material benefits. There was the story of an award-winning sculptor encountering Rákosi at a public reception. 'What are you doing at the moment?' Rákosi enquired. 'I'm trying to learn table tennis', replied the sculptor. Why was that? 'Because if I become a champion, I would then be granted a passport and permitted to travel.' Such was the envy for sporting prowess.

Watching in Helsinki was Stanley Rous, secretary of the Football Association and 10 years later to become President of FIFA. He was so impressed that he immediately arranged for the champions to come to Wembley for a friendly the following year. This occasion, more than Olympic victory, sealed for Hungarians for all time their sense of lasting honour. England were still regarded as among the foremost if not the leading nation – widespread though suspicion of vulnerability to foreign technique might be. They were the glittering prize: never defeated at home, other than once by the Republic of Ireland in a match at Goodison Park, Liverpool. It is hard to imagine today the significance of that event, on a misty day in London, for the comparatively tiny population of a central European state under the yoke of Soviet repression. Hungary's victory by six goals to three, more of a rout both morally and technically than the score suggests, was a landmark in the history of football. Those of us present – including many of the future coaches in domestic English football such as Ron Greenwood, Malcolm Allison and Dave Sexton – were astounded by Hungary's flexibility. As the Football Association's *Yearbook* reported, Hungary's performance had 'almost geometrical accuracy and ball control amounting to elegance … they overcame the traditional continental weakness in finishing and shot four of their six goals from outside the penalty area'. Of Hungary's six, Hidegkuti scored three: when England travelled to Budapest the following summer in preparation for the World Cup, the rout was worse; they lost 7-1.

Commentators far and wide viewed Hungary as inevitable winners of the World Cup staged in Switzerland, the only doubt being the score. Convictions strengthened when they rattled home 17 goals in the first two games: nine against South Korea and eight against a strategically weakened West German side, whose coach Sepp Herberger deliberately shielded his true formation from Hungarian analysis. A key to the trophy's destination was the bad injury suffered by Puskás in a tackle by Germany's centre half Liebrich. He left the field, there then being no substitutes, and missed both the quarter-final, a temperamental punch-up with Brazil, and also the semi-final against Uruguay. At his own mistaken insistence, Puskás returned for the final against full-strength West Germany. He was way below par, and Hungary went down 3-2. A seemingly legitimate late equaliser by Kocsis was disallowed for marginal offside by an English linesman. The greatest of all teams had surrendered the prized trophy to Herberger's shrewd tactics. In Budapest, 10,000 roamed the streets and cafes in prolonged despair. Some even demonstrated outside the apartment of manager Gusztáv Sebes – angry that he had dropped Budai (a key figure in earlier rounds) in order to restore a half-fit Puskás.

And that, more or less, was the end of Hungary's mystical XI. Honvéd for two seasons continued to be the team to beat: when they lost a friendly against Wolverhampton Wanderers, the British press mantle of 'World Champions' bestowed upon Wolves provoked UEFA, under encouragement from L'Equipe of France, to introduce the European Cup for 1955–56.

In 1955 Rákosi, having conceded office to Imre Nagy,

retaliated with a campaign by the Working People's Party to denigrate Nagy for right-wing deviation. This led to an anti-government, anti-Soviet uprising in the autumn of 1956, at which time Honvéd were on tour. A number of players including Puskás, Kocsis and Czibor declined to return home. The latter pair joined Barcelona, and the itinerant Puskás ultimately signed for Real Madrid. There he enjoyed a partnership with former Argentinian Alfredo Di Stéfano, unparalleled to this day, as sensational in its impact as anything witnessed during Hungary's golden years.

▲ **1** London 1908: Britain's women, led by gold medallist Miss Sybil Fenton 'Queenie' Newall, dominated the women's Archery tournament. Of the 2,008 competitors at the 1908 Games, only 37 were women.

▼ **2** London 1948: The Opening Ceremony of the 'Austerity Games' which marked the start of the BBC's first extensive Olympic Games coverage. The BBC's 64 hours of programming were watched by an estimated audience of 500,000.

▲ **3** London 1948: John Mark, a
22-year-old medical student and
president of the Cambridge University
Athletic Club, lights the Olympic Flame
at Wembley on 29 July 1948. The final
torchbearer's identity had been kept
secret, but his 'Greek god' good looks,
to personify Youth and Vitality,
helped to secure his selection.

▲ **4** Sydney 2000: Cathy Freeman lights the ring of fire at the magnificent Opening Ceremony in Sydney, a landmark moment for the Aboriginal people. The Games proved a great success and delighted the Olympic and Paralympic Movement.

▼ **5** Munich 1972: Gold medallist Mary Peters celebrates her Pentathlon victory on the Olympic podium. She is flanked by Heide Rosendahl of West Germany (left), who took silver, and Burglinde Pollak of East Germany, who won bronze.

◀ **6** Beijing 2008: Oscar Pistorius, the Blade Runner from South Africa, in full flight during the Paralympic Games where he won three gold medals. Three years later Pistorius was to run the qualifying time for the 400m for the Olympic Games at London 2012.

▲ **7** Sydney 2000: Matthew Pinsent leads the impromptu celebrations for Steve Redgrave's fifth gold medal on Penrith Lakes. It was to be Redgrave's finest hour and his last ever Olympic race.

▶ **8** Paris 1924: Eric Liddell, the Flying Scot, in characteristic athletic pose, his head back as if exalting in his own speed. Liddell won the 400m, his least favoured event, in a world record time and also took the bronze medal in the 200m.

▲ **9** Beijing 2008: In Cycling the men's Team Pursuit epitomised the slick excellence of the all-conquering British squad, breaking the world record in the Laoshan Velodrome.

▼ **10** The triumphant Pursuit team (from left Paul Manning, Ed Clancy, Geraint Thomas and Bradley Wiggins) display their gold medals.

▶ **11** Seoul 1988: Britain's Stephen Batchelor and teammates celebrate one of the three goals which beat West Germany to win the Hockey gold medal. The amateur team also scored a memorable semi-final victory over Australia.

12 Beijing 2008: Troy Sachs was the talisman of the 'Rollers', the Australian men's Wheelchair Basketball team, who defeated the 'unbeatable' Canadians in the final. The only survivor of Australia's gold medal winning team from 12 years before, Sachs described the cohesion between his new teammates as 'a bond of steel'.

13 Munich 1972: wreaths laid outside the Athletes' Village in Munich commemorate the deaths of 11 Israeli athletes and officials. This grim outcome marked the end of innocence for the Olympic Games.

The Golden Amateurs

Seoul 1988
Barry Davies

For one glorious moment, field hockey became Britain's national sport and a team of part-time players became household names

The question is, why should so many people, the vast majority of whom knew little or nothing about the sport of hockey, have set their alarm clocks to be ready for the start of the final on television – at 6am on Saturday 1. October 1988? The participants on that memorable day, in the Songnam Stadium in Seoul, South Korea, still can't quite believe they did.

The simple answer, of course, was the hope of a gold medal for the Great Britain men's Hockey team to bring the total won by the country at the Olympic Games of 1988 to five. But I believe that there was more to it than that. For here was a band of men who counted among their number a quantity surveyor, a newsagent, a hospital registrar, a bank clerk, a transport manager, two school-teachers and an RAF PT Officer who, helped no doubt by the increasing media coverage, had touched a chord with the nation.

It would be absurd to say they played for fun, but their sport began as their weekend pastime. Now, as they learned to live with growing expectation, survived moments of doubt to benefit from them, and achieved their collective aim of being the best, there was, as many of them said later, a greater satisfaction being successful as part-time sportsmen. They were gifted amateurs with a thoroughly professional approach in the days when both expressions were complimentary.

But success was a long time in the making and owed much to political intervention. In 1980 when the Prime Minister, Margaret Thatcher, followed the lead of the President of the United States, Jimmy Carter, and called for a boycott of the Olympic Games in Moscow because there were Soviet troops in Afghanistan, the Great Britain Hockey Board concurred. Their team, all prepared, was withdrawn. In 1984, Britain's Hockey record was judged as only good enough to be first reserve for the Games in Los Angeles. But then, with paper-thin concerns about security, Leonid Brezhnev, the President of the USSR, played the spoilt child and said to the Americans, 'you wouldn't come to my party so we are not coming to yours.' Leaving historians to decide which of the two political acts was the more futile, the British Hockey team seized their chance with relish. With seven survivors from the team denied their opportunity in Moscow, they arrived unbeaten in the semi-finals, lost there by the only goal to West Germany and came home with the bronze medal.

Since December 1978 the team had been managed by a man from the world of finance, Roger Self, who was not one to court popularity or seek compromise. He called a hockey stick a hockey stick, knew precisely what he wanted and would have no truck with petty officialdom or the political in-fighting among the home nations. But he inspired his men and treated them as adults. Nor would he have cared a jot that it was not until 1 October 1988, on a warm sunny afternoon in Seoul, that everyone in British hockey became his friend.

He had done it his way, and that included choosing as his coach one of the players who, eight years earlier, had waited at Heathrow in his Olympic blazer in the departure lounge offering nowhere to go. Coming to the international role without club experience David Whitaker, a schoolmaster at Marlborough, would prove that while you teach, you learn yourself. His quietly determined manner led to occasional clashes with the more obviously combative Self, leaving Bernie Cotton, who would have been captain in Moscow and was now assistant manager, to calm the waters. But the leader and the tactician would prove a perfect foil for each other and their mutual respect was a cornerstone of ultimate victory.

Willesden in north-west London was the setting for the next part of the story, with nine of the team from the Los Angeles 1984 Games adding silver medals to their bronze as England finished as runners-up in the 1986 World Cup. For the public, initial curiosity was fanned by coincidence; and the crowds that grew to capacity – unprecedented for hockey – were well rewarded.

Just three months on from the magnificent Azteca Stadium in Mexico City, I found myself perched in a wooden box in a tree with a rather closer view of England against Argentina than in another World Cup. But there was no 'hand of god' here, nor call for English supporters to boo: just a victory that exactly reversed the football score – 2-1 to England. Then, in a semi-final not the final, and 20 years on from the FIFA World Cup that had taken place just 14km down the road at Wembley Stadium, England played West Germany. England again wore red.

Again there was a late goal that took the match into extra time at 2-2; though this time it was England who equalised. And again England won. Paul Barber's penalty corner was the decisive goal, though Germany's Michael Hilgers hit Ian Taylor's left-hand post as the hooter blew and the crowd celebrated. They knew it was all over. Next day, what had been a balmy autumn gave way to winter rain, and Australia won the final. But, maybe, some of the moments lingered on in the mind.

Self was only an observer at Willesden as the England team had their own manager, Colin Walley, but Whitaker was again the coach. All but one of the GB team that played at Los Angeles 1984 would move on to Seoul; Norman Hughes, who had joined the 100 caps club, losing out to Father Time. He was already 33. Four others joined the squad: Martyn Grimley, Robert Clift, Imran Sherwani, who missed 1984 through injury, and David Faulkner, who, two decades later, has played a huge part, as GB and England Performance Director, in leading the hockey revival that seeks gold in London 2012 for both men's and women's teams. Veryan Pappin, the Scottish goalkeeper, and the Irish defender, Stephen Martin were retained for their second Olympic Games, with a second Irishman, Jimmy Kirkwood, and an extremely gifted 18-year old Englishman, Russell Garcia, a hairdresser from Havant (now Scotland's coach), completing the squad of 16.

There would be a few ups and downs in the two years' build-up, including failing to win a match in the annual Champions Trophy in Lahore in the March of the Olympic Year. Self tried enough players to fill two squads, and the pressure applied on those chosen to be single-minded in their collective task was unrelenting. Their families were required to understand, and their employers cajoled into giving them increasing time off work. At one stage Self dropped his most experienced defender, Paul Barber, designed surely to send a signal not only to him but also to the team as a whole. But then when they arrived in Hong Kong for final preparations, much of it was done on the golf course. The team were ready, and on arrival in the Olympic Village clearly buoyed by the fact that Ian Taylor, their lion of a goalkeeper, would carry the Union Flag in the Opening ceremony.

As second seeds GB made an auspicious start with Sean Kerly scoring his 50th goal for his country in the opening match with South Korea; a lead doubled four minutes into the second half. But Self's warning to his team to beware of treating the match against the hosts played on the second pitch as 'a pitch two game' was, seemingly, not heeded. From two up, it ended 2-2; and his clear irritation at being asked to explain a brief spat he'd had with Kerly over a substitution, made for an uncomfortable evening. Worse would follow when, after a win over Canada, came defeat by Germany. The winning goal, at 2-1, was a penalty stroke in the last minute when Barber was adjudged to have deliberately cleared a flick shot in the circle with his stick above shoulder height.

The expressions of the British players made it clear: they thought the dream had died; that it had been taken away from them. But they were wrong on two counts: first, the decision by the Australian umpire, as they later admitted, was technically correct if very harsh; second, the dream was still theirs to control. Canada had drawn with Russia, so winning their last two group matches – against Russia and India – would mean a place in the finals.

Self frequently told his team that you are only as good

as your next match, never the last one. His other dictum was 'all or nothing', and that now concentrated the collective mind wonderfully well. At least it did until Kerly gave GB a 2-0 lead 10 minutes into the second half of the semi-final against Australia. But with celebration came a lowering of the guard, and within 20 seconds Australia halved the deficit. The balance of the match changed: with 13 minutes left, Australia – the tournament favourites – equalised.

What happened then is as clear in my memory as the final. I was a spectator; Nigel Starmer-Smith was at the microphone. Looking perhaps to see his reaction to his goals being wiped out, I caught an image of Kerly's face as irritation quickly gave way to resolve. He would claim later that fatigue was his motivation, the dread of extra time. But having now enjoyed his company in and out of the commentary box for many years, I have learned that the fighter on the pitch is a self-effacing man never conceding that he was a very special player. It seemed he was to be denied when a shot destined for an unguarded gap at the far post suddenly became a legbreak, and bounced on by. But with three minutes left, as Kulbir Bhaura struggled to control a pass in the circle from Richard Dodds, Kerly seized the moment. From further away from the ball than either Bhaura or the Australian goalkeeper and at full stretch he completed his hat-trick and won the day. The sort of goal, as Self remarked, that only Kerly could have scored.

With their place in the final won, Self gave his team an evening on the town courtesy of the BBC. It was an excellent evening, though the bill gave the producer an ashen face for some time. The slight hope that such largesse might allow a camera on the team bus going to the final didn't materialize – it was never going to! But the thought was a compliment to their status now in television's eyes.

I can't recall a moment in the final when I doubted that Great Britain would win. With Dodds, the captain, giving the lead and Jon Potter alongside ever available, there was a calm authority about their play. As the shrewd Whitaker put it, 'we were determined to give nothing away and dictate the pattern.' They did so with style. All three goals were well made and came at good times: after 20 minutes, early in the second half, and with 13 minutes to go. The crisp and often early use of the ball from the back and midfield to an attack brimming full of pace and trickery was the key. Stephen Batchelor, down the right, had a fine match setting up the goal chances for Sherwani, who snaked through defenders for the first and clinically put away the third. In between, Kerly took his tournament tally to seven when at a penalty corner the Germans were expecting the firepower of Barber.

The scenes afterwards were wonderfully chaotic, but the fact that it was ages before the Victory Ceremony took place gave the players the chance to really enjoy their win. There were cameos everywhere: a gracious bow by the winning team to the colourful Korean supporters who came every day in their finery; Richard Leman, now President of the GB Hockey Board, leaping up and down with Kirkwood chanting 'we gave them a bloody good hiding', then lifting the diminutive Minister of Sport, Colin Moynihan, high in the air; the wives and sweethearts rushing to be photographed on the medal podium; the Princess Royal calmly walking through the growing crowd, offering congratulation with genuine pleasure. And all while cameramen and journalists sought to capture the scene or elicit the quote of the day: Kerly later admitted to feeling a pang of sympathy for the Germans, who had lost consecutive finals; Sherwani talked of the reward for all those exhausting runs up Trentham Hill (near Stoke-on-Trent), and Whitaker spoke for everyone with the comment, 'a moment encapsulated in my life which will never disappear'.

Like the players who only fully appreciated what they had achieved and what the country thought of them when they saw the crowds waiting to greet them at Heathrow, I only learned of the reaction to my comments about the third goal when I returned home. Thinking how the speed of the attack had found the German defence absent without leave, I said, 'where were the Germans?' And then I thought does it matter; GB have the gold now, for sure. So I added, in the flush of anticipated victory, 'but frankly, who cares?' People have been very generous about it ever since, and I'd like to think that in a small way it helped convey to the viewers a feeling of what it was like to be there on that memorable day. For those who perhaps did care, for I concede my words were just a little biased, I should record that Germany made the final score 3-1.

Total Eclipse of the Track

Beijing 2008

Brendan Gallagher

Led by Chris Hoy and the Pursuit team, the all-conquering British Cycling squad reached perfection in the Velodrome

Perfection, by definition, is both rare and elusive, but you always know the instant you have witnessed it. For three minutes 53.314 seconds at the Laoshan Velodrome at the 2008 Olympic Games we looked on open-mouthed as the GB Team Pursuit squad went to work. There are, as the song tells us, nine million bicycles in Beijing, but none had ever been ridden like this before.

It was hypnotic and beautiful to watch, as aesthetically pleasing as it was physically extraordinary, a definitive snapshot of flawless execution under extreme pressure. It was a performance that left even Sir Steve Redgrave, watching high on the gantry, shaking his head in awe; a moment that redefined what mankind can do on a bike. Perfection is meant to be what sportsmen aim for, not what they achieve. The wonder is that it happens at all. But one of the many beauties of the Team Pursuit is that it encourages perfection because, though the latter stages of the event are straight knockout – two teams on the track, racing against each other – the real race is against the clock. Everything the riders do in training and in racing is defined by fractions of a second. And the clock is ever measurable, ever constant. So take a bow Ed Clancy, Paul Manning, Geraint Thomas and Bradley Wiggins.

The GB squad broke the world record in their winning ride that afternoon, and provided the 'ideal' metaphor – one hesitates to use the word 'perfect' again – for whatever genius or magic it was that had transformed Britain into cycling's superpower. Britain left Beijing with seven gold medals from the track programme while Nicole Cooke and Emma Pooley added gold and silver respectively in the women's road events. The 'Great Haul of China' as more than one newspaper headlined it.

The triumph of the Team Pursuit squad might have looked ridiculously easy as they nearly caught the crack Danish team in the final, but that's the strangest thing about perfection: it can appear inevitable, pre-ordained and unstoppable. Don't be deceived: the GB quartet that day in Laoshan had pushed themselves to the limit in the build-up and had made great sacrifices, personal and professional, to reach that state of grace. On gruelling winter and spring training camps on the windy mountainous roads of Majorca, seven hours a day on the road was nothing unusual. Every third day they beasted themselves up and down their 'favourite' eight-minute climb for three hours until they were left crumpled by the roadside, helped off their bikes and driven back to their hotel by the GB coaches.

There was not a hill to be seen in the Laoshan Velodrome, unless you counted the steep 47-degree banking, but that massive workload from their training in Majorca was precious money in the bank. It built up the endurance and resistance to lactic acid that the foursome needed to think clearly when maintaining inch-perfect control at speeds of more than 65kph. Wiggins and Thomas, the engine room of that team, had also completed the 3,500km Giro d'Italia earlier that summer on top of their Majorca sessions and those marathon efforts helped them to dig deeper still.

And of course there had been endless track work, refining their skills and unity as a quartet. First, they peaked for the World Championships in Manchester that March, when they broke the world record, and from mid-June they never spent less than three hours a day together on the track, perfecting those glorious soaring swing-ups and spectacular descents to within a couple of inches of the furiously spinning wheel ahead. One particular training routine used to take my breath away every time. It involved the full six-man GB training squad in a rolling 3km session at about 80 per cent effort. But the choreography was different. Instead of the front rider pulling away and swinging down from the banking onto the back of the line, he had to swing down into the gap between riders five and six. There was maybe 15cm to spare either side, certainly no more, often less. The move required incredible bike handling and machine-like accuracy.

A few of the top riders will tell you that sometimes, once settled in the line, they actually like to feel the lightest of touches on the wheel in front of them because then they know exactly where they are rather than just guessing to the nearest few centimetres. To the amateur that sounds like complete madness, but we are talking about the crème de la crème here, professionals who operate on another plane. In my eyes, the Team Pursuit remains the most glorious sight in all Cycling, a visual and emotional feast.

For the GB squad in Beijing, every rider had a precise role. Ed Clancy always led off; his job was to get the team somewhere near their cruising pace of 67kph by blazing away for one and a quarter laps before swinging up to allow 'captain' Manning through. Clancy redefined the role of the lead-off man: a rider with blazing speed not far short of a Chris Hoy, but with the endurance and resistance to lactic acid to return to do further turns later in the race and then hang on for grim death to the finish. Though less heralded than others, Clancy was actually the man who revolutionised the GB Pursuit Team. Once he perfected the start, their times started to tumble down.

Manning, the number two man, had a brutal, unenviable job. His task was to hang on to Clancy as best he could and then nudge the speed up to maximum, setting the pace and cadence for the rest of the ride. While Clancy and Manning blazed away, Thomas and Wiggins were trying to relax and get a 'tow' before their huge stints at the front. In theory, their slipstreaming saved 30 per cent more energy than fighting the wind at the front, but it did not always feel that way.

In smooth motion, the British team resembled a runaway train rattling down the track. Four carriages moving as one, linked by imaginary couplers. Lean together, move together, think together, win together. No words were spoken, no breath wasted. This train was on autopilot. The trick is never to let the speed drop, because the effort to accelerate and regain that speed takes you into the red zone. You will blow a gasket in the final kilometre. This is an exact science, a mathematical equation that cannot be contradicted even by the fittest of bodies. If you feel yourself slowing you have to swing up and let the next man through. This train waits for nobody.

The focus on movement is total. No stopping, no brakes, no glass to break or emergency cord to pull.

Concentrate on that wheel a couple of centimetres in front of you, swing up again, nail that sweet spot on the banking – the spot where gravity dictates that the bike wants to plummet down more than it wants to keep going up. Get it right and it's like creaming an off-drive through the covers, misjudge it by a fraction and you are edging the ball down to third man. The margins are minute, there is no room for error.

The rhythm is almost seductive. Swing down, back into line, head down, tuck in, concentrate, work on those aerodynamics. Head down, shoulders tight, elbows in, back flat, butt down. Watch that front wheel again, I said watch the front wheel again. Breathe, you must remember to breathe. Right concentrate, try and relax, two laps respite before you have to do a big turn again. Swing up, swing down, swing up again…

Down by the track Dave Brailsford, the Team Manager, punched the air in delight and high-fived all and sundry as the GB squad flashed across the finishing line. Even he had to let it all out after a ride like that. Throughout that epic week in Beijing, Brailsford had maintained an almost Zen-like calm amidst the media mayhem, although a contented smile was rarely far from his lips. Steadfastly he refused to tempt fate. In fairness, his riders were 'only' achieving what he had always felt deep inside they might achieve. While the rest of the sporting world may have been gawping with astonishment, he wasn't particularly surprised.

Admittedly, seven gold medals was freakishly good but he had always reckoned on four or five gold medals. Moreover, the team had miraculously suffered no illness, mechanicals or crashes, the bad luck you would normally expect at such a high intensity five-day Olympic meeting.

The GB squad had arrived at a point when anything other than that level of success would have been a massive disappointment.

The previous evening, with the echoing Velodrome long emptied, the Team Pursuiters were quietly warming down after smashing the world record in their final qualification ride with a 3:55.202 ride when Brailsford joined a few lingering press to shoot the breeze. You got the feeling he didn't really want to leave the track at all. Never the boastful sort, he did eventually head back to the Olympic Village, leaving us with a parting shot, 'If you thought that was good, you ain't seen nothing yet, just wait until the final tomorrow.'

Brailsford's squad were all-conquering in Beijing, but it hadn't always been like that. For decades Britain were bit players in the Track Cycling world, well behind Australia, France, Germany, Holland and the old Eastern bloc. The occasional exceptional individual – Chris Boardman at Barcelona 1992 and Jason Queally at Sydney 2000 – bucked that trend, but it was only when lottery funding started to kick-in after 1998 and Brailsford imposed his own unique management style on the GB squad's elite performance programme that the picture changed dramatically.

A useful amateur cyclist in his time, Brailsford is more a manager than a coach. His genius is for assembling and motivating the necessary experts, inspiring them to move in the same direction. He sees the bigger picture but is also consumed by micro-management. He is famous for his 'aggregation of marginal gains' philosophy, which is actually much simpler than it sounds. Do 100 simple small things as well as you can in a complicated process and, all other things being equal, you are likely to be more successful than your opponent. In Yorkshire they have another expression that covers much the same ground, 'If you look after the pennies the pounds will take care of themselves.' It's just a matter of when you cash in.

By the Athens 2004 Games, the GB squad was becoming much more competitive across the board with golds for Wiggins in the Individual Pursuit and Chris Hoy in the Kilo and a silver medal in the Team Pursuit although the latter came home a disappointing three seconds behind the Australians. They had hoped for much better.

From that platform, however, Brailsford went in to overdrive and the handling of the Team Pursuit squad was indicative of the approach taken in all the Olympic disciplines. Trusted lieutenant Shane Sutton was put in charge and the riders and management formed the 3:55 Club. The sole purpose of the club was to produce a squad that could ride the 4km Team Pursuit in 3:55, which they thought would be more than sufficient to win a gold medal in Beijing. The club included equipment boffins such as Chris Boardman, who turned to bike design after retiring as a rider; sports scientists, the so-called number crunchers; conditioners; physiologists; coaches; psychiatrists and, of course, the cyclists themselves. They would meet regularly – once a month, sometimes more often – to plan and plot how it could be done and how training could be tweaked. Brailsford even commissioned a motivational video that lasted exactly 3 minutes, 55 seconds.

There was more. The so-called Secret Squirrel Club, headed by Boardman, was also beavering away, finetuning the bikes and aerodynamic race suits and helmets and pushing the regulations of the Union Cycliste Internationale (UCI) to the limit. There was a satisfying element of cloak and dagger. The UCI, like most governing bodies, distrust radical change, so every time the GB team introduced an innovation they did it unannounced and quietly videoed the unsuspecting UCI scrutineers passing their bikes fit for purpose. If at some date in the future – say 5 minutes before an Olympic final – the GB bikes were called into question, the team could provide conclusive evidence that the exact same bike or piece of equipment had been recently passed by the same UCI scrutineers. Not everyone within the sport was happy with this ruthless approach, usually those trailing home in second place.

On occasions the GB squad would elaborately hide their bikes under covers to enhance the air of mystery. Much of the time there was a deal of kidology in all the secrecy. With Boardman at the helm, GB riders were never going to have anything less than top quality equipment, but were they really so far ahead of the game? If the opposition are even thinking such negative thoughts, the battle is already half won.

Talent spotting was something else at which the GB team excelled. Rower Rebecca Romero had won a silver medal in the Quadruple Sculls at the Athens 2004 Games, but had fallen out of love with her sport and craved an individual gold medal. Brailsford swooped and four years later she was, remarkably, the women's Individual Pursuit champion. Former World BMX Champion Jamie Staff, who had been trying his hand with mixed fortunes at the Keirin and Kilo, was suddenly switched to the lead man in the Team Sprint, where all his extraordinary power could be harnessed to maximum effect. Staff could cover the first lap in just a fraction over 17 seconds from a standing start, transforming GB from medal contenders to Olympic Games champions and world record holders.

And of course, as luck would have it, Brailsford was

blessed with some awesome, once-in-a-lifetime natural talent within the team. To have one rider of the quality of Vicky Pendleton, Bradley Wiggins or Chris Hoy was rare, to have three at once was astonishing. Between them the trio won four individual gold medals, six in total. Not that Hoy's magnificent haul of three gold medals was entirely plain sailing. When the UCI scrapped his gold medal event, the Kilo, after 2004, the big Scot faced a distinctly uncertain future. It turned out to be the making of a great champion as Hoy turned to other events to unleash the full range of his power.

Initially Hoy's aim was simple, to earn a place in the Team Sprint squad, but then, impressed by the new speed he was finding and encouraged by the GB coaches, he wrenched himself right out of the comfort zone and started competing in a few Individual Sprint and Keirin events with startling results. Gold medals in both disciplines quickly followed at the UCI Track Cycling World Championships. At the age of 32, the real McHoy re-invented himself as the fastest sprinter in the world. Add to that an unflappable temperament and you have the basis for what he achieved in Beijing: three gold medals and victory in all his 18 races. It all looked so easy and unstoppable, as once-in-a-lifetime natural talent was backed up by supreme teamwork and an attention to detail that was new to the sport. And it worked – heady days indeed. Opponents, some of them very big names indeed, appeared to roll over as if complicit in their own downfall. In fact they were simply outclassed, bypassed, by a team in pursuit of perfection.

The Rock of the Rollers

Beijing 2008
Gareth A Davies

Australian legend Troy Sachs destroys the aura of Canadian invincibility

The Beijing National Indoor Stadium is in uproar. The venue is packed to capacity with a largely Chinese audience, entranced by the culture shock of Wheelchair Basketball. A small section in the stands, Australian flags waving, bounce up and down with glee, banging their feet on the floor. Australia have just pulled off one of the most improbable victories in the Beijing 2008 Paralympics Games, dethroning Canada who many had nailed down for a third successive gold medal. The scenes of jubilation are merited. The men's Wheelchair Basketball gold medal is the toughest team title in Paralympic sport – bar none.

Sixteen men, down on the court, pump their fists to the heavens and squeeze the air from each other's lungs, in embrace, like heroes returning from mortal conflict. The score, 72-60, belied the game. It was close. Very close. Several of the players are in tears. Australia have come full circle. They will return home with the gold medal for the first time in 12 years. They won in Atlanta 1996, yet suffered the ignominy of fifth place at Sydney, their own backyard, four years later. They had come back to take silver in Athens 2004, beaten by Canada, always by Canada.

Yet it is Canada whom they just have played off the court in Beijing. Canada, who were heading for a third title after winning all seven of their games in Beijing, including a dramatic 69-62 semi-final victory against the United States. Canada, who are led by Patrick Anderson, the LeBron James of Wheelchair Basketball; who had led the Canadians with 33 points, 21 rebounds and six assists. Yet this game had been meticulously planned and beautifully executed. The sages had said Canada were unbeatable. They were wrong.

The dirty dozen from Down Under thought, felt and knew differently, in spite of the Canadians having dominated the sport for eight years. For 'The Rollers', as the Australian team was known, had in their ranks veteran Troy Sachs, who had won gold with Australia 12 years earlier. The sole survivor from that team, Sachs was the talisman, a player who had revolutionised the sport and influenced young players around the world, including the Vancouver basketball star Anderson. This gold medal match symbolised the older master taking back what he believed was rightfully his. But what Anderson, the world's leading player, hadn't banked on was the way the canny Australians shut his teammates – not him – down in the final.

Sachs has always been cool and calculating. Behind the scenes, the Australians knew they had the formation capable of creating the upset. It was all based around strength in depth, in teamwork and resolute defence. In the 2008 Beijing Paralympic Games tournament forward Justin Eveson was averaging 19.6 points a game and shooting at 65 per cent from the field, while team captain

Brad Ness was hitting 18 points a game at 53 per cent.

Up to that point, centre Sachs had only averaged 5.4 points a game, spending large parts of the tournament in foul trouble (in danger of being sent off). But his mobility, fitness and desire in the final, along with Eveson and Ness, proved to be crucial. Australia knew that the Canadians relied heavily on Anderson, who had racked up an average of 20.1 points a game, shooting at 51 per cent from the field.

Early in the match, Canada had started to reel the Australians in. From 16-10 down, the team took advantage of Eveson's enforced absence on fouls. Sachs came on. He played most of the match. When David Eng slotted a big three-pointer with 20 seconds left at the end of the first quarter, it put Canada ahead, 17-16. The Rollers struggled in the second quarter, as Anderson and Joey Johnson kept the score ticking over for Canada. Canada led 32-28 at half-time. Four points down and one half to go.

Australia made their move in the third quarter. Eveson crucially stayed out of further foul trouble and The Rollers made the most of it. Good shooting and strong defence put the pressure back on Canada, and by the last break Australia were seven points clear. Panic rippled through the Canadian ranks, and in a frantic final quarter Australia played the percentages. With a minute remaining, Australia were five points up, Canada on the attack. When the shot missed, Eveson hurled the ball down court for Sachs to roll into the basket and score. Canada grew desperate, took wild shots and began fouling. Australia pushed the lead out to 12 points as the final minute ticked down, by hitting five free throws and a lay-up.

Anderson was the game's highest scorer with 22 points,

yet centre Sachs, in a dream denouement before retirement after five successive Games (which started aged 16 and had earned him a silver and two gold medals), hit 19 points as top scorer for the newly-crowned Paralympic champions. The old master had gazumped the younger man who had once idolised him. Aussie teammates Justin Eveson and Shaun Norris combined for 33 points, and centre Ness had a game-high eight assists. Team captain Ness and Sachs broke down in tears as the final hooter sounded. Anderson had scored 10 of Canada's 13 in the last quarter. The only other field goal came from his assist, one of six. Australia's game plan of marking the other players in Canada's team had paid off handsomely.

Canada, relinquishing their title, undoubtedly had the world's star player in Anderson. Yet in the final 40 minutes of play, on the penultimate day of the Beijing Games, he had been upstaged by a group of Australians who had signed a secret pact 10 months earlier that they would accept nothing less than the gold. Second – or 'first last' as it is known Down Under – would not be good enough.

Since 2000, Canada had set the benchmark for the world to follow. Silky skills, epitomised by Anderson. Conversely, Australia's style of play was built around power. From 2002 onwards, Australia had found the right blend of players. But wheelchair basketball is often about development, teamwork and fluidity. Momentum is also huge in the sport.

At the Athens 2004 Paralympic Games, Australia had accepted that they would lose to Canada in the final. They simply needed to mature. Looking back on Athens, Sachs now believes it was a mistake. Yet, going into Beijing, the Australian team had made their pact: nothing less than gold. When they lost matches in the group stage, they let it go. The only aim was quarter-final qualification.

At the heart of it all was Sachs. He carries a name not unfitting of a gladiator – in which many ways he was. Standing 1.93m tall, weighing 90kg, he had burst onto the scene at the Atlanta 1996 Games as a 20-year-old, revolutionising the sport with his novel moves, individual skill and an aggression bordering on intimidation. Australia had beaten Great Britain 78–63 to seal the gold medal, with Sachs stacking up 42 points in the Final. I was there. And he was on fire in that match. Diego Maradona at the 1986 FIFA World Cup; Ian Botham in the 1981 Ashes series; scrum-half Gareth Edwards in the 1970s in the red jersey of Wales. Add Sachs in his pomp to that exclusive band.

Troy Sachs was born without the shin bone in one of his legs. The leg was amputated at the age of two and a half and he has worn a prosthetic since then. Sachs played soccer until the age of 14, when a sports development officer came to his school and asked him if he wanted to try wheelchair basketball. He'd found his metier; he was brilliant, skilled and dedicated. Aged 16, Sachs headed off to play in the USA, where he went on to represent the Dallas Mavericks. He later played in Italy and Germany and has even played recently in Turkey, before retiring. At the Beijing 2008 Games, he was a veteran, aged 32, wily, yet determined to restore Australian pride, a totemic character, the glue that bound the team to that gold medal a dozen years earlier.

In Beijing, the talisman was called up for a major role in the final because a teammate was in foul trouble. In Atlanta, it had been very different; Sachs had changed the way the game was played. 'I started to tilt the lyrics there,' he recalled. 'I pushed it as hard as I could. I was 20 years old, was 6ft 4in tall and I liked to throw my 90kg around. I had no fear. I also started tilting my chair on the side to gain height, I think I brought an able-bodied mentality to a disabled game and I think the team sort of followed. It brought an admiration from people or disgust from people ... it was all about winning.

'Around the world it did make people like a young Patrick Anderson sit up and go "wow, I could do this for a living". He carried on that tradition. They're all modelled in my image, as in aggressive, play hard and focusing on your team and not really worrying about the opposition.'

Sachs and the Australian team were a drilled unit. They had a unity of thought. There are five players on the court, but Australia had a saying from 12 months out, articulated by Sachs: 'Sixteen in the team: twelve players and four support staff.' It didn't matter who was on the court, no egos, no grandstanding, it didn't matter who scored 50 points, or who scored two points, or who stopped the basket. If every player did his job, they would return home with the gold.

In January 2008, there was a 'test' event in Beijing for Wheelchair Basketball. The pollution and smog had forced 'ten out of the twelve' in the Australian squad to use asthma inhalers and do chest exercises, according to Sachs. When the Games proper arrived, the factories had been switched off for several weeks. 'We got the better end of the climate and the environment to perform in.'

Typical of the Australian way, they just prepared hard. Unlike other nations, like the British squad, there was no boot camp. Instead, they endured gruelling training sessions and pushing sessions. The bonding was done around a table, chatting and quietly talking about why they wanted to win gold medals, why they wanted to see the flag raised, why they would commit themselves to pain and sacrifice.

'It was more mental than physical,' explained Sachs. 'We'd already formed a bond of steel on the practice court. Our practices were full on, harder than any of the matches we took part in at the Games. You know the old adage: control the ball and don't worry about anything else. The basket is at 10 feet tall, the court is ninety-four feet long. The ball will bounce. If you put the damn thing in the hole more times than them, you win.'

By the time the Beijing 2008 Paralympic Games arrived, Sachs was more of a mental player. His role in the team was 'insurance', as the group referred to it – to come on and provide the third brain in the three-headed monster with Brad Ness and Justin Eveson. Yet in the Final, Eveson was in foul trouble after eight minutes. It meant Sachs played most of the final. It was the perfect stage for the big game player. Sachs could not have signed off a glittering Paralympic career in a more telling manner.

Sport sounds simple, sometimes. Sachs recalled the entire team had all their energy and wits about them. 'I was confident in what we were going to do. I guess we ran away with it in the end, because we had put a chink in their armour, and their team under too much pressure. They weren't used to it. They didn't know how to respond, and that's what happened. Anderson was flashy, tough, but when push comes to shove, when he's under pressure in big games, he seems to falter.'

The half-time team talk, with the eventual champions four points down, epitomised the drilled Aussies. No panic. The coach, Benjamin James Ettridge, said two sentences: 'points on the board' and 'let's all do our jobs.

Put in 3 per cent more, and the game is ours.' He gave no rousing speech. 'There wasn't anything like that,' recalled Sachs. 'I guess that was one of the things I quite liked about the final in '96. We were total underdogs. It was about slogans and sayings and a clear game plan in 2008. We had a quiet confidence about our form and what we could do and if we did those things we were really, really confident that we could win the gold medal.' So it proved.

The aura of invincibility built up over two gold medal-winning Games slipped away from the Canadians as Australia pulled off one of the most thrilling gold medal victories ever seen in Paralympic sport.

'Such sporting drama was soon to be overwhelmed by the horror that was to take place outside the arena'

Murray Hedgcock, journalist and eyewitness at the 1972 Olympic Games.

4

THE SHADOW OF MUNICH

Munich 1972: Tragedy and triumph

Tragedy and triumph

Munich 1972

Murray Hedgcock

The day that terrorists struck at the heart of the Olympic Games

The report I filed on Saturday morning, 26 August 1972, made the lead in the Sydney *Daily Mirror*. 'Armed police are guarding the gates and patrolling the roads of the Olympic Village, to prevent any political demonstrations marring the opening of the 20th Olympiad.

'Security all over the Olympic Park has been drastically tightened in the past 48 hours, with hundreds of plain-clothes police everywhere. There is unease that Black Power demonstrators or émigré groups, including fanatical anti-Communists, may seize the opportunity for demonstrations.'

The dispatch reflected the mood of tension and apprehension before the opening of the Munich 1972 Games. The world was nervous, we were nervous and our hosts the most nervous of all. I was wrong in my report, but not by much. Nothing was to happen then, but, 10 days later, the Games would explode into an eruption of politically motivated violence, bringing images that would horrify the world and shake the Olympic Movement to its foundations.

Many had asked before the Games if it might be too

early to give Germany, which was still rebuilding mentally and physically after the ravages of the Second World War, the honour of staging the world's greatest sporting event, the most visible coming-together of nations. And did the Germans themselves want the fierce spotlight of international attention shining on their country? Yet there was hope that the Games would bring a fresh start, not just for Germany, but also for the whole Olympic Movement.

Germany and the romantic Bavarian capital of Munich had organised carefully and effectively. The determination to look as un-threatening as possible was apparent in the uniforms of the Olympic Village security guards. Mostly students, they wore floppy caps and two-piece suits, in a cosy shade of powder blue. The attendants at the media quarters, and our coach drivers, were reticent young army conscripts who appeared to enjoy the switch from the parade ground. Not all the foreign media felt well disposed towards their hosts. But with a German wife I was sympathetic, and found it an agreeable and stimulating setting on arrival, three weeks before the Games opened. Most of the media, both from my own group and competitors, flew in with the team some days after I arrived.

There was an immediate good omen in the sight of Jesse Owens at the Media Centre, working as a commentator with United Press International. You do not need to be an Olympics buff to know of Owens's impact at the Berlin 1936 Games. He won four gold medals for the United States: the 100m, 200m, Long Jump, and 400m Relay. It intensely annoyed Adolf Hitler, who expected the Games to demonstrate the superiority of the Aryan race, but was forced to confront the fact of a black man defeating whites. Now, in 1972, Owens was back in Germany, welcomed by all, busy, lively, and happy to forgive, even if he could never forget. His autograph is a treasured souvenir of the man and his achievements, written neatly on an Olympic dining-room napkin.

The Munich 1972 Games continued the steady postwar expansion of the Olympic Games, bringing together 7,134 athletes from 121 nations. They contested 195 events from 23 sports, including for the first time men's Indoor Handball, Slalom Canoeing and Kayaking. And an old discipline was revived – Archery – after an absence of 52 years. The Olympic Park, built on an abandoned airfield, was dominated by the imaginative Stadium with a partial roof, almost futuristic in its styling.

My reporting base was at this magnificent Stadium, the venue for the track and field, the true heart of the Summer Games. They opened to plan, and there were few results to make headline news, whatever their impact on followers of the individual sports. Two swimmers dominated the headlines: Mark Spitz and Shane Gould. The American Spitz won seven golds, the most achieved by an individual athlete at one Games in Olympic history, while Gould, a 15-year-old Australian schoolgirl, won three golds, one silver and one bronze. And the world fell in love with the impish Russian gymnast, Olga Korbut, astonishingly a team reserve only called upon because a now-forgotten teammate was injured.

Telephone calls back home (a bonus on overseas assignment, as the office pays) brought a different perspective to the restricted world of the on-the-spot reporter, concentrating on major sports rather than the esoteric world of gymnastics.

'What do you think of Olga Korbut – isn't she extraordinary?' came the question from London one night.

'Never heard of her. Who is she?' was my justifiable

response. And when the astonishing global impact made by television coverage of the talents and charm of the tiny Russian became apparent, it was a sharp reminder that there is no guarantee that attending a sporting event guarantees you the best view. Korbut, just 17, and looking years younger, starred as the Soviet women gymnasts won their sixth straight Olympic title in the Team Competition. Korbut added two individual gold medals and one silver, which helped the Soviet Union head the final medals table with a tally of 99.

The rivalry of East and West Germans was intense, but remained under control, the crowd generous in its applause when the muscular Renate Stecher took the women's 100m and 200m for the East, beating Australia's Raelene Boyle into second both times. The long-legged 16-year-old schoolgirl Ulrike Mayfarth sent the West German crowd into ecstasy as she took High Jump gold, while Britain's lovable Mary Peters stunned the watchers by snatching Pentathlon gold from home favourite Heide Rosendahl – unmistakable for her spectacles and trademark red socks. Rosendahl had already taken gold in the Long Jump and added another in the 100m Relay. Meanwhile, a bearded Finnish policeman, Lasse Virén, recovered from a fall to set a world record as the crowd shouted him on in the 10,000m; he also won gold in the 5,000m. But such sporting drama was soon to be overwhelmed by the horror that was to take place outside the arena.

Eight members of Black September, a Palestinian terrorist group, climbed the Village fence around 3am on 5 September, helped by American athletes who assumed the group were competitors returning late from a night on the town. They forced their way into the block occupied by the Israeli team, two of whom were killed, although others managed to escape. Ironically, the Israelis had gone into Munich the previous evening to see the play, *Fiddler on the Roof* – set in the time of anti-Jewish pogroms in Tsarist Russia. The terrorists demanded the release of 200 Palestinian prisoners in Israel, under the threat of killing one hostage every hour if this was not agreed by noon.

Negotiations began with IOC members Willi Daume of Germany and Ahmed Touny of Egypt, Olympic Village mayor Walter Tröger, and Munich's police chief, Dr Manfred Schreiber. Chancellor Willy Brandt flew to Munich to take charge. Federal Interior Minister Hans-Dietrich Genscher was later to reveal that he had offered himself as a hostage in exchange for the Israelis.

The Israeli government stood firm. The deadline was extended several times, as the drama was played out under the probing eye of television, new satellite technology taking continuous coverage to more than 900 million viewers in 100 countries. The BBC scored a coup as it had an office overlooking Connolly Strasse, the street housing the Israeli block, and commentator David Coleman drew a vast audience as he reported, hour upon hour.

Most sporting events were cancelled for the day, but a handful went ahead after much debate, particularly those contested away from the Olympic Park. Australia was drawn against West Germany in the men's Basketball at an outside hall. The coach taking the Australian team was parked outside the closed-off Village, and I was able to join it. Play went on with no one knowing what was happening back in the Village, both teams throwing themselves into hectic activity that for the moment took our minds off the drama. Australia won 70-69.

With nothing like mobile phones, Twitter or other new

media technologies to keep us informed, we left the coach outside the Village and waited as police and troops directed operations. It was early evening. The spotlights of police helicopters were breaking the gloom as they clattered only a few metres above our heads – a bizarre experience.

Eventually the Basketball players were given the all-clear to walk into the Village. All were in official Australian team uniforms except for myself, clutching a player's sports bag as cover, and staying well inside the group – at 1.75m, surely the shortest international player in the history of the game.

But inside the compound, there was little news. Here again was the hazard of the news reporter, able only to be in one place at one time. People back in Britain watching television knew far more than we did, but nowhere could we find the BBC transmission. After 15 hours, the hostages, blindfolded and bound with torn bed-sheets, with their captors, were driven in an army bus through the underground car park to two waiting helicopters. The agreement was that they would transfer at the German air force base of Fürstenfeldbruck to a Boeing 727, to be flown to Cairo, where negotiations with Israel would resume.

Soon after midnight, the IOC emergency session was told – no one appears to know on what authority – that the hostages were safe, and the terrorists killed or captured. This welcome news was rushed round the world by the hundreds of journalists monitoring the drama: Europe went to bed, persuaded of a satisfactory outcome. At 3am those of us inside the still-closed Village were called to a press conference in a big bare room. We stood in a circle around a group of politicians, police officers and Olympic officials, to be told in stunned silence by the Bavarian

Interior Minister, Bruno Merk, that all nine hostages, five terrorists and a policeman had been killed.

Reporters shouted their protests at the early misinformation; no one could explain it. On this grim Munich morning, hardened journalists were unusually quiet as we went to our offices to file our shockingly updated reports.

It was months before the full detail emerged. It appeared that the German authorities had totally bungled the rescue attempt at the airfield. Police had begun shooting before a proper plan of campaign had been set in motion, and tragically the terrorists reacted by murdering all their hostages.

Should the Games continue? Public opinion was divided sharply between those who felt it wrong to continue with anything as peripheral to life as sport, and others insisting the terrorists must not be allowed the victory of killing the Munich 1972 Games. The athletes were split. Many felt overwhelmed by the tragedy, losing any motivation to compete: others, single-minded in pursuit of what could be the biggest event in their lives, closed their minds to outside concerns, and wished to carry on.

Willi Daume, President of the Munich Organising Committee, wished to cancel the remaining programme, but other IOC members, led by the 85-year-old IOC President Avery Brundage, of America, preferred to continue – a stance endorsed by the Israeli government. A memorial service was held in the main Stadium on the following day, before 80,000 hushed spectators and 3,000 athletes. The show was to go on, however sombre the mood.

Munich had not quite finished for me. On the night of Saturday 9 September, journalists joined the Australian team in a long-planned *bierhall* dinner as a Games farewell, where we tried to forget the dreadful events three days earlier. Midway through the evening, word came of new trouble in the Village, involving at least one death. My colleague Ray Kerrison, head of the News Limited New York bureau, and I rushed to the scene. Officials were tense in the wake of the massacre, and armed police moved into the complex, to reports of shots being heard. No one was allowed inside; so Ray and I bypassed security by simply walking in through the exit to the underground car park.

We got in around midnight – to be picked up within minutes by the Village guards. We were escorted to an office, had our media passes removed, and were left to wait. The Australian team's German liaison officer was contacted: he arrived eventually, vouched for us, and we were politely ejected from the Village, with the advice that we should not try similar subterfuge again. We didn't. The security scare was a tragedy of Games high jinks, an Austrian student being killed in a fall when climbing a flagpole, seeking to take a flag as a souvenir.

I went home on the Monday after five hectic weeks in Munich. My last memory of the Games has stayed always – of walking behind two sleek characters in the airport departure lounge, each bearing over his shoulder a suitbag, marked in large, clear letters: 'U.S. Secret Service – White House'.

It was a moment to wonder: had the West quite come to terms with the message of Munich, and the need to face up properly to the new threat of organised terror? And it was a reminder that a much more covert and overt security presence would be increasingly essential in Olympic and Paralympic Games to come, as the Movement, founded with such high idealism, lost more of its innocence.

'Tell him about the times when war did not separate us and tell him that things can be different between men in this world'

Luz Long, German Olympic athlete, in his last letter to Jesse Owens, 1942.

5

'WINNERS' IN DEFEAT

London 1908: The Most Famous Collapse

Berlin 1936: Brothers in Arms

Sydney 2000: Marla's Inner Vision

The Most Famous Collapse

London 1908
John Goodbody

How Dorando Pietri lost a gold medal but won eternal fame

There was pandemonium in the White City Stadium. Out on the track, the Italian runner Dorando Pietri staggered a few metres and then collapsed again. When he rose once more, he seemed unable to focus on the track, probably only remembering the words he had said before the race, 'I will win or I will die.' His hands were clasping corks (used by many runners to keep their hands closed), his face looked gaunt and strained. His legs buckled under him again as he weaved his way onwards towards the invisible tape. Saliva was round his mouth as the public watched the grim agony of the runner. Marathon running was in its infancy and most of the spectators had never seen an example of such human heroism, just to win a gold medal.

Dorando Pietri both sparked a boom in long-distance running and became the first international hero of the Olympic Games. His collapse just before the finish of the Marathon at the London 1908 Games brought the Olympic Games global recognition and gave meaning to the words spoken that year by Baron Pierre de Coubertin, known as the father of the Games, who famously said, 'What is important in life is not victory but the battle. What matters is not to have won but to have fought well.'

These sentiments have become the credo of the Olympic Games, but it was the Italian runner from a small village in northern Italy who so dramatically and, because his suffering was preserved on camera, so graphically brought De Coubertin's words to life. Although Spiridon Louis had won the first Olympic Marathon at Athens 1896, the impact of his victory, the highlight of the Games, was felt far more in his native Greece than it was internationally, largely because the Games were relatively undeveloped and unpublicised in 1896. However, the drama of the 1908 Marathon resonated on both sides of the Atlantic. And there was little in Pietri's previous life, apart from the frequency with which he had collapsed in races, to suggest that he was to become the first hero of the Olympic Games in an episode that is still remembered more than a century later.

Born in Correggio, outside Carpi, in northern Italy on 16 October 1885, the young Dorando worked initially as an apprentice in a clock and watch repair business but then moved to become a delivery boy, carrying chocolates to the burghers of the district, a task that he made more arduous by sometimes running to his destinations with the packages. He competed in cycle racing in his youth and reputedly first became inspired by running when he defeated a leading Italian athlete, Pericle Pagliani, over 10,000m. In 1905, after winning a road race in La Spezia, covering 22.4 miles in the astonishing time of 2 hours 5 minutes, he was first in an international Marathon in Paris. However, he failed to finish in the Intercalated Games in Athens in 1906 and also in another Marathon in Italy that year, as well as in the trial event for the 1908 Olympic Games, held on 7 June, less than seven weeks before the Marathon in London. In those days, having two such demanding races so close together was not considered inadvisable.

Pietri stayed in the Soho Hotel in London for the Games and he spent some time writing to Teresa Dondi, his girl-friend (and subsequently his wife, who outlived him and died in 1979). In interviews with Italian newspapers, Pietri later recalled: 'I knew I had formidable adversaries but I didn't let that put me off. I was going to run my race without worrying about other people's tactics. I relied a lot on lung power and can assure you that when I attack the uphill parts of a course, I seem to have four lungs instead of two.'

The course was from Windsor to the White City, the new Stadium built with remarkable speed and efficiency in West London and only demolished in the 1980s to provide for the expansion of the BBC offices. Prior to this race, there was no established Marathon distance. The race began on the East Terrace outside Windsor Castle under the windows of the royal nursery, following a request from Princess Mary, so that her children could see the start. It was also determined that to give more spectators a chance to see the race at close quarters inside the Stadium, 385 yards of the circumference of the track should be run, decisions that would have significance not only for Pietri in that race but also for the future of the Marathon. From 1924, the distance of 26 miles 385 yards became the established length of the event.

The race was started by Lord Desborough, the President of the Organising Committee and one of the most versatile sporting figures of the age. He rowed in two Boat

Races, represented Oxford in the Varsity athletics match, twice swam across the Niagara, was three times punting champion of Britain, won a military fencing tournament, and was also an excellent shot and an Alpine climber. He was also a friend of King Edward VII and the support of royalty was essential to the success of the Games.

Pietri's rivals were manifold. Apart from the Britons, running before their own crowds, there was Charles Hefferon of South Africa, Tom Longboat, a member of the Onondaga Nation who ran for Canada, whose amateur credentials had been questioned, and also John Hayes, one of the Irish-American production line of outstanding athletes based in New York, who were to dominate the Hammer and the Shot Put in the early Olympic Games. As a youngster, he had been helping to dig subway tunnels in Manhattan, which may have been a useful mental preparation for the rigours of the Marathon, but gave him little time to train. The Irish, like the Jews, looked after each other in the United States and Hayes was found a 'job' in Bloomingdale's, a department store, where he was given plenty of time off to train. He was second in the 1908 Boston Marathon, finishing so strongly that a local paper described him as 'being as fresh as a daisy.'

When the London 1908 Marathon started, the temperature was over 25°C and many of the runners, including Pietri, wore a knotted handkerchief on their heads, although the weather was cloudy for much of the race. The local paper, the *Windsor Express*, raised concerns about possible drug-taking, which was a worry even in those early days of the Games, although some of the products used, such as strychnine, seem extraordinary in retrospect. Strychnine may have stimulated the central nervous system, but it could be fatal.

Buoyed by the enthusiasm of the occasion, the British competitors went off too fast, with Scotland's Thomas Jack leading for the first five miles, only to drop back. Then another Briton, Jack Price, took over. Longboat threatened for a while but retired and Hefferon went into a commanding lead. With just over six miles left, he was nearly four minutes ahead of Pietri, who had worked his way through the field and was closing on the South African.

Hefferon then made a crucial error, accepting a glass of champagne from a spectator. This upset his stomach and he slowed, allowing Pietri to overtake him. If Pietri had then adopted a steady pace, he might have won but he pressed on. As he said later to Italian newspapers: 'I was seized by a fury to go ever faster. I pushed myself until I had no one else challenging me. With the road ahead clear of me, I could not put a brake on myself. The runners passed between lines of spectators on both sides. I could not see them but I heard them.' What was heard was the firing of cannons to indicate to the spectators inside the Stadium that the first runner was in sight. However, outside the White City Stadium, Pietri was suffering. He saw the grey-coloured arena but said later he remembered very little afterwards. When Pietri came down the Cycling track, surrounding the Athletics track, he clearly was in an exhausted state. He turned the wrong way but officials blocked his path and indicated the right way. Then he collapsed on the track.

The spectators, including Queen Alexandra, were distraught. Here was the first man in the event unable to complete the final few yards for victory. They screamed for him to be helped, not realising that this would risk his disqualification. However, Dr Michael Bulger, the Medical Official, who had won an Irish rugby cap in 1889, helped to haul Pietri to his feet. The official report points out, 'It was impossible to leave him there, for it looked as if he might die in the presence of the Queen.'

After he had collapsed for the fourth time, there was a huge shout from the other side of the Stadium. Another runner had entered the White City Stadium. This was not, as had been expected, Hefferon but the American Hayes. The crowd was still urging on Pietri, who, as he was about to collapse for the fifth time, was still surrounded by officials and a policeman and being nursed by Dr Bulger. It was then that Jack Andrew, the principal organiser of the event, put aside his vast megaphone and, escorted by Dr Bulger, virtually carried Pietri over the line. His time was 2:54.46. Hayes, looking remarkably fresh, finished 32 seconds later.

As Pietri was carried away on a stretcher, Andrew announced, 'First and winner of the Greek Cup, Dorando Pietri of Italy.' And his name was inscribed on the blackboard and carried round the arena. The Americans protested and after about an hour – all the officials were British – the result was altered with Hayes being announced as the winner. However, it was Pietri's struggle that was remembered by spectators and by Arthur Conan Doyle, the author of the Sherlock Holmes stories, who was reporting the Games for the *Daily Mail*. He recalled many years later: 'No Roman of the prime ever bore himself better than Dorando of the Olympics of 1908. The great breed is not yet extinct.'

However, the drama of the day was not yet over. At about 10pm the Central News Agency put out a report that Pietri had died, only to correct the news 90 minutes later. By the following morning, Pietri was telling everyone that he could have finished the race unassisted, although this was evidently not true, especially given the fact that the Italian later admitted that he could not recollect what happened inside the Stadium.

However, the occasion was still to be cherished and Lord Desborough suggested to Queen Alexandra that she should present a cup to Pietri. This she duly did later that day, with a card stating 'For Pietri Dorando [sic], In remembrance of the Marathon Race from Windsor to the Stadium. From Queen Alexandra.' The Americans, somewhat miffed that the victory of Hayes had been overlooked in all the drama, carried the champion out of the arena on a table.

The race immediately triggered a fascination with long-distance running and a boom in professional races, especially in the United States. In Britain, a massive trophy was presented by the *Sporting Life* newspaper to find a British athlete capable of wiping out the shame of the Marathon in the London 1908 Olympic Games, in which no home competitor finished in the top eight, let alone won a medal.

Across the Atlantic, Pietri defeated Hayes three times in indoor races, although he was beaten in turn by Longboat and other runners as for a short time the circuit became very lucrative. Dorando's brother and manager, Ulpiano, was a prime mover in cashing in on the popularity. However, by 1910, interest had collapsed. The brothers opened a hotel in Carpi that soon closed and Dorando was left virtually destitute.

But Pietri was a survivor in life as much as Athletics. He became a taxi-driver, attracting customers through his legendary status and was employed by the Italian Athletic Federation to identify young talent. Pietri had had his moment in the sun and everyone wanted to be driven by the man who had brought Marathon-running and the

Olympic Games to international attention. He died of a heart attack in 1942. He was 56 years old.

If Dorando had only slowed down when he approached the White City Stadium that fateful day in July 1908, he might have won Olympic gold. If he had, only the occasional athletics enthusiast would have remembered his name. As it is, by his courage in adversity, he became the man, who perhaps more than any other athlete, pioneered the popularity of the Olympic Games.

Brothers in Arms

Berlin 1936
Craig Lord

*The moving story of a sporting friendship that lasted
two lifetimes*

Along the road from Catania in Sicily, beyond a stone
tablet framed with bougainvillea and engraved 'Deutscher
Soldaten 1939–1945', the echoes of battle whisper of
wisdom learned from more than one field of engagement.
Among the 4,561 German lives lost on the island during
the dying days of the Second World War and commemo-
rated in the quiet cemetery of Motta Sant'Anastasia is a
tale of heroism and friendship of epic proportions.

As the roar of guns and blast of bombs launched by the
approaching Allied Forces grew louder in early July 1943,
the thoughts of Luz Long, a 30-year-old lawyer serving as
a senior Lance-Corporal with the German army, strayed
back seven short but troubled years to a singularly important moment of sportsmanship: in a thronging Berlin
1936 Olympic Stadium soaked in swastikas and sullied by
propaganda, the European Long Jump record holder and
Leipzig law student had defied Adolf Hitler by embracing
a symbol of all that the Nazis had set out to destroy.

Long would never know that a note he wrote to his friend
Jesse Owens from the front in 1942, just after the United

States had declared war on Germany, had reached the star of the Berlin 1936 Olympic Games, an African American athlete whose race and colour spelled inferiority under Third Reich doctrine. Ridiculed for relying on 'black auxiliaries', the USA team was also scorned by one German official for allowing 'non-humans, like Owens and other Negro athletes' to compete.

Owens shot all of that down in flames with athletic superiority worth its weight in more than the four gold medals he won, the message reinforced through the very public friendship that Luz Long initiated during the Long Jump competition in front of a 110,000-strong crowd that stood to welcome Hitler with a mass Nazi salute. It was a question of a master athlete and a worthy competitor humiliating those who believed in a master race.

Reflecting on his own act of defiance in the face of brutality and discrimination as an athlete from Leipzig (a city that would rise up in 1989 and spark the collapse of the Berlin Wall and unite a divided Germany that he would never know), Long, husband and father, risked much in 1942 by penning what would turn out to be a prophetic and haunting request:

'My dear friend Jesse,
My heart is telling me that this is perhaps the last letter I will ever write. If that's the case, I beg one thing of you: when the war is over, please go to Germany, find my son Kai and tell him about his father. Tell him about the times when war did not separate us and tell him that things can be different between men in this world.

Your brother, Luz.'

The Olympic silver medallist, who was born the year before Germany initiated the First World War, was wounded during the Allied invasion of Sicily on 10 July 1943. Four days later (some records suggest three days), Carl Ludwig 'Luz' Long lost his life in a British-controlled military hospital at San Pietro Clarenza and was buried at Motta Sant'Anastasia, where Albert Schweitzer's words hang heavy in the air: 'The soldier's graves are the greatest preachers of peace.'

In 1951 Owens, in response to Luz's request, sought out and met Kai Long and told him that the friendship he had had with the boy's father was the most valuable treasure he had kept from his Olympic experience.

The drama that played out in 1936 as Hitler watched is to this day widely cited as the prime example of how sportsmanship can triumph over the ugliest forms of competitiveness. What unfolded between Long and Owens and the message it sent to the wider world transcended athletics and stretched to global politics as the storm clouds gathered for one of the darkest periods in human history.

In the athletic context, Owens had punctured the myth of an Aryan super race long before he arrived in Berlin. On 25 May 1935, the son of a sharecropper and the grandson of slaves leapt 8.13m at Ann Arbor to set a world record that would survive 25 years and 79 days. The official programme and subsequent approved reviews of the Olympic Games, one sponsored by a Hamburg tobacco manufacturer, shed no light on that stunning performance: the 7.98m leap of Japan's Chuhei Nambu from 1931 was the world record according to Nazi Germany.

The thumbprint of Nazi censorship is visible on every page, the official report records 'the Wonderful Fight' as follows: 'The German starts off with a 7.73 leap, while Owens suffers a foul jump. After that, the Leipzig student manages a wonderful jump that shows his strong fighting spirit and the public rewards him with spontaneous applause: 7.87, the loudspeaker announces as Luz Long matches the "USA Wunderathleten". The cheering refuses to die down as Owens gets ready for his second jump. Before he goes to the runway, he smiles at Long and congratulates him. He then storms down the runway and a moment after he leaves the board he lands far in the depth of the pit: 7:94!! Long puts all his efforts into his last attempt but misses the board. Owens in the meantime confirms his victory with a final jump of 8:06. That marks the first time in Olympic competition that the 8m mark is broken. His performance demands our singular admiration and Germany is proud to have put up a competitor who demanded the very best of Owens.'

In 1935, the Nazi regime effectively created two types of Germans: 'citizens of pure race' and 'subjects' to 'protect German blood and honour'. Tall, blonde, blue-eyed and athletic, Luz Long embodied the very idea of 'Aryan', while Owens was just about as remote from Hitler's fantasy as was possible. The contrast was described in a 1936 report of the French sports newspaper *L'Équipe* as follows: 'Long, the typical Aryan, blonde locks tumbling on to his forehead, honed body, robust, battling against a black man under surveillance.'

References to the sequence of events on 4 August 1936 vary a touch in the telling, but there is little dispute over the way the result of the Long Jump unfolded. In preliminaries a day after he had won the 100m on the track and on the same morning as the rounds of the 200m, Owens was reminded that he would be granted no leniency. Still in a sweater and tracksuit bottoms, he took a practice run down the runway, leapt, landed and rose to his feet to find that his effort had been counted as his first jump. Rattled, Owens fouled his next attempt too and was a jump away from being eliminated.

Enter Luz Long, the European record holder. He approached Owens, extended his hand and introduced himself. The precise words exchanged by the men have gone to the grave, but it is widely reported that Long advised Owens to make a mark well shy of the board and aim for that as his take-off point because he only had to clear 7.15m to qualify for the final and could do so with some ease. It was the confidence boost that Owens needed: he took off some 45cm away from the board and cleared the cut-off by just 1cm.

The final was held under the gaze of Hitler later the same day. Owens set the tone with a leap of 7.74m and followed on with 7.84m and 7.87m. Long jumped 7.54m, 7.74m, 7.84m, 7.73m and then, on his fifth leap, registered 7.87m to send the patriotic crowd into a frenzy. The cheering had not abated as Owens prepared to go again. 'He leaned over for the first time close to the ground, sprinted like we had known him to sprint in the 100m, and leapt, a bird for a moment ... 7.94!' reported L'Équipe.

Long was the first to rush over to congratulate Owens, who would later utter words long-since immortalised in history as symbolic of the spirit of the Olympic Movement: 'It took a lot of courage for him to befriend me in front of Hitler. You can melt down all the medals and cups I have and they wouldn't be a plating on the 24-carat friendship I felt for Luz Long at that moment. Hitler must have gone crazy watching us embrace.'

Perhaps even more so when he witnessed the

magnificent conclusion to the competition as summed up by one of the American sports writers there that day, Grantland Rice: 'As he hurled himself through space … Owens seemed to be jumping clear out of Germany.' At 8.06m, a stunning moment caught by Leni Riefenstahl's team for her Nazi-approved documentary of the Games, Owens proved himself a class apart. Long fouled his last attempt before the top two finishers walked arm-in-arm off the field towards the dressing rooms.

Hitler did not present the medals nor did he ever congratulate Owens, the star of the Berlin show. Instead, he cowered near the athlete's exit so that he could shake the hand of the German athlete who had made the de rigueur Nazi salute on the rostrum. One evening in the Olympic Village, Owens and Long met for a private talk, according to some accounts. It was the last time the two would ever meet, though the connection between the athletes survives to this day.

At the 2009 World Athletics Championships in Berlin, Kai Long, then 70, and his daughter, and granddaughter of Luz, Julia-Vanessa Long, and Marlene Dortch, one of Jesse Owens' granddaughters, shared a platform in memory of a friendship formed in the same Stadium in 1936. Kai Long recalled meetings with Jesse Owens in 1951, 1964 and 1978, the first of those the moment when Owens repaid the kindness shown to him by Luz Long by honouring the deceased athlete's last request to him. 'We met in 1951. Jesse Owens came with the Harlem Globetrotter basketball team,' said Kai Long. 'We met in Hamburg. He was dressed very smartly. He came to see if I would come there.'

As part of the celebrations, Owens ran a lap of honour in the 1936 Stadium in front of 80,000 cheering fans. At the end of it he was greeted by the Mayor of West Berlin with the words, 'Jesse Owens, 15 years ago Hitler would not greet you or shake your hand. I will try to make up for it today by taking both of them.'

In 1964, Owens returned to Germany for the filming of the documentary *Jesse Owens Returns to Berlin*, in which he recreated that lap of honour for the cameras. It was a poignant moment for an ageing athlete. 'I had many thoughts as I ran,' said Owens, who dedicated his memoirs to Luz Long. 'As I passed each section, there was a bridge to the past. I passed that platform of champions where four times I stood to receive the gold medal ... the sounds of the past are in the walls and the archways and the very ground I am standing on, for here time has always stood still.'

If that is all captured on film, then the 1951 meeting of Owens and Long junior is caught in photographs that have been donated to the German Sports Museum in Berlin. In 2009, when Kai Long was asked his thoughts on the courage it took for his father to help and befriend Jesse Owens on 4 August 1936, he replied: 'I think it is not a question of race, black and white. It's about the spirit of the amateur athletes, the action of the clean amateurs. I was told it was absolutely about that in amateur sports: to help each other. What my father did probably happened several times during the 1936 Olympics. But Jesse, of course, said it was a fantastic thing that his opponent was ready to help him through the qualifications ... This was a little spark. Not an action, but a little fire lit by Jesse Owens ... this fire got brighter and brighter and is still burning. There was no action, it just happened. All I know is what family and friends told me. It was a normal occurrence in sport.'

Against the backdrop of 1936, it was also, arguably,

the greatest gesture in the history of sport.

Long, bronze medallist at the European Championships in 1934, continued to compete after the 1936 Games, and in 1937 recorded a lifetime best of 7.90m. He finished law school that year and practised briefly in Hamburg before all healthy men were drafted to fight for the Nazis. He did so until that fateful July day in Sicily.

The story of Luz Long will not fade with time, so resonant is its message to humankind. Yet there remains deep contrast between the way the two men who shook hands and formed a friendship in defiance of Hitler back in 1936 have been treated in the intervening years.

Years after the 1936 Games, Owens was asked about 'the Hitler snub' and replied: 'When I came back to my native country, after all the stories about Hitler, I couldn't ride in the front of the bus. I had to go to the back door. I couldn't live where I wanted. I wasn't invited to shake hands with Hitler, but I wasn't invited to the White House to shake hands with the President, either.' Things would be different by the time he died.

In Berlin, a street leading to the Olympic Stadium is named Jesse Owens Allee – the great athlete's family having attended the dedication ceremony as guests of the German government in 1982, two years after Owens, a smoker, died of lung cancer. In tributes to Owens, US President Jimmy Carter said: 'Perhaps no athlete better symbolized the human struggle against tyranny, poverty and racial bigotry. His personal triumphs as a world-class athlete and record holder were the prelude to a career devoted to helping others. His work with young athletes, as an unofficial ambassador overseas, and a spokesman for freedom are a rich legacy to his fellow Americans'.

In 1990, President George H.W. Bush posthumously

awarded Owens the Congressional Gold Medal, calling his victories in Berlin 'an unrivalled athletic triumph, but more than that, a triumph for all humanity'.

Perhaps time will be kinder to Luz Long too. In Germany to this day, there is scant official recognition of a man posthumously awarded the Pierre de Coubertin medal, or True Spirit of Sportsmanship medal, by the Olympic Movement. The Leipziger Sport-Club 1901 for which Long competed has no track and field athletes these days, tennis, hockey, football and snooker being the only sports represented. While Long's medal and some of his personal possessions and letters are preserved at the Leipzig Sports Museum, there is no sports hall, no stadium, not even a long jump strip named after him. Long has never been awarded any German prize nor is there one named in his memory.

In Leipzig, you can wander along Luz Long Weg and peer over a hedge at an athletics track. That remains the only honour afforded to one of the central characters of the 1936 Games by his – and the host – country.

Marla's Inner Vision

Sydney 2000
Kate Battersby

Declared legally blind at the age of nine, Marla Runyan still found her way into Olympic Games history

Marla Runyan still wonders what might have happened if she had sat in the pack and kicked with the rest of the field. But it wasn't in her nature to be like the rest and the pace was slow, so she had taken the lead earlier than she had planned – only to be outrun on the final lap. It didn't help that she lost her bearings in the middle of Stadium Australia. She thought there were 600m to go when just one lap remained. But, in a sense, nothing mattered by then. Whether she finished first or last in the final of the 1500m, the journey had already been completed. She was an Olympian.

'It was momentous, yes, this gargantuan experience, but I felt a simultaneous certainty that it was just a moment in time that would pass,' recalls Runyan. 'The pursuit of the thing was more important than the thing itself.'

When, at the age of nine, Marla Runyan's mother told her she was legally blind, her reply was simple: 'No, I'm not.' One way or another, that thought carried her all the way to the final of the 1500m at the Sydney 2000 Games. All her adult life she had told herself she was an

Olympian. She could not see, but her focus was absolute. She won multiple golds at the Paralympic Games, but still wanted more. Her dream was made reality at 31, when she became the first legally blind athlete to compete in the Olympic Games.

Runyan herself has long become used to the questions. 'What do I see? I've been asked that question since I was small … I have an edge of peripheral vision that, although cloudy, is enough to let me negotiate a world-class footrace. I can see people's feet. I can see the colours of my competitors' uniforms. I can see the red track surface, and the waving of flags, although not which nations they represent. I just can't see the finish line. When I run a race, I don't always know if I've won or lost. I only know that the finish is at the end of the straight.

'People wonder how a woman who is only partially sighted can race at middle distance in world class company … especially if you've seen me drag my nose across a page with a magnifying lens cradled in one eye, or watched me narrowly dodge a parking meter that's in plain sight. My answer is: when you run as fast as I do, things tend to be a blur anyway.'

Marla Runyan was born in January 1969, the second child of a bank teller. She recalls her childhood in the relentless glare of the Californian sunshine as plain hard work. Able to see normally in infancy, her increasing visual problems went undiagnosed until she was nine, leaving her with memories of white coats and cold steel medical equipment and other unpleasant devices – tongue depressors and pin lights and eye charts. It took eight months to reach the correct diagnosis: she had Stargardt's disease.

This degenerative condition affects about one in 15,000 people. The condition leaves holes in the delicate, light-sensitive membrane in the back of the eyes that absorbs and translates images. Runyan was left with a slim band of peripheral vision, and even that was flawed and needed correction. But her central vision was not correctable. She started spending a lot of time outdoors because 'there I didn't feel blind. I felt like the fastest kid in the world'. At 11 she took up the high jump and eventually competed at State level, despite seeing the bar only in the last moment before her feet left the ground. Football (of the Association variety) was another favourite. Unable to see the ball, she worked out where it was from the way the others chased it.

'I genuinely thought that outdoors my vision was normal. It never occurred to me that other people were seeing things I wasn't seeing.' Her mother, Valerie, called it the Great Illusion, the way in which Marla almost convinced herself the legal blindness didn't exist. Runyan granted herself no favours. In a sign of what was to come, she became determined to learn the way all her classmates did, by reading. 'I suspected if I gave in to my vision on the smallest matter, I would be tempted to give in to it on the larger matters for the rest of my life,' she explained. 'I didn't want to humour my blindness. I cultivated denial as a protection from the temptation to become a victim.'

But, as she says now, she made her life more difficult than it already was. There was a difference between accepting limitations, which she still refuses to do, and accepting the basic condition and making peace with it. 'I wasn't the most approachable kid. My secret was becoming my trap. I walled myself up, and resented it when I was misunderstood.' But nothing got in the way of her determination, and she even learned to drive.

Only when she went to college, San Diego State, did

she start to receive any formal athletic training. During the Seoul 1988 Games, Runyan became fascinated by the legendary Jackie Joyner-Kersee's performance in the Heptathlon, and took up the event, including the 100m hurdles. As she observed, 'The key is rhythm. I couldn't see the hurdles, but I knew how to get over them.'

In 1990 she attended the World Disabled Championships. In her autobiography, *No Finish Line: My Life As I See It*, Runyan recalls staying in an old military base where the food was awful, the nights freezing cold and every one of her races was run in the rain. Nevertheless, she found the efforts of others profoundly inspiring. Her Heptathlon personal best was just 300 points short of the 5,500 required to make the USA team for Barcelona 1992, but by then she was studying to become a teacher of deaf and blind children, and the workload was too much. She went to the Barcelona 1992 Paralympic Games, 'to give myself a consolation prize – and gave myself one of the most meaningful gifts I ever had. Everywhere I looked, an athlete was doing something which made my own impairment look relatively minor.' She won gold in the B3 – most sighted blind category – 100m, 200m, 400m and Long Jump. Yet Runyan didn't want only to compete in the Paralympic Games – she yearned to be an Olympian.

The US Olympic Trials for the Atlanta 1996 Games became her goal, but she was punishing herself with so much work and training that her performances suffered. She thought sleep and rest meant laziness, and only later realised, 'If all you do is train without rest, you don't build. You break.'

Her performance at the Olympic Trials – the only route by which any American athlete can qualify for the Games – was a huge letdown, with the exception of the final event, the 800m, which proved to her that she should concentrate on middle distance. Such was her focus on the Olympic Games that her autobiography omits to mention that she won two more medals (a gold and a silver) in the Paralympic Games that summer.

Yet, for all her struggles until then, this last Olympiad before the realisation of her ambition would be her toughest. She moved to Eugene where the temperate Oregon climate suited her much better than the California glare. She learned the biomechanics of running, and realised that what she had previously regarded as her own mental weakness was not that at all. She simply needed to alter her training to become a faster runner.

Several seasons of injury frustration followed. She barely raced for two years. Then, in just the third 1500m of her life, she qualified as part of the US team for the 1999 IAAF World Championships in Athletics in Seville. She made the final and was disappointed to finish 10th. But at last, at the age of 30, she had sponsorship and could be a full-time athlete. For the first time, 'everything I did, every mile I ran, every hour I slept, every meal I ate had to have a purpose'.

A knee injury almost ruined her preparation for the crucial US Olympic Trials in 2000, but somehow she made them, and then the team. 'Nothing hurt any more. I was an Olympian.' It was in many ways the peak of her achievements. The Games themselves would be an anticlimax by comparison. Yet she loved the atmosphere among 'the elite of the elite, and I never got tired of being in that company'.

Nerves in the first round saw her scrape into the Semifinals. She barely made the Final, and while others thought she could win a medal, Runyan never believed it.

She ran the final in front of 110,000 people in Stadium Australia, finishing eighth, but even in the build-up to the most important minutes of her competitive life, the reality seemed merely strange. 'Maybe I could have held on for a medal. Or not.'

After Sydney she moved up to the 5000m, qualifying for the Olympic Games in Athens four years later, but going out in the first round. She was 35, and it was time to focus on other things. In 2005 she had a daughter with her coach and husband Matt Lonergan. She now works as a communicative disorders specialist and, as might be imagined, as a motivational speaker. Her words rarely fail to impress, as she recalls her childhood and the ambition that took her to two Olympic Finals.

'I don't run for medals, although I've won my share. Running to me is freedom from confusion and obstacle. It is liberation from the medical terminology that has slowed me down since I was a child. Running is freedom from the sedentary and the stagnant. When I'm about to run a race, I can hear people whispering, "Oh, there's a blind girl running. Isn't that great?" But I believe you can be more disabled by your attitude than by vision loss.

'Indoors I was impaired, because I strained to read a book or see a television, or even know who I was talking to. But when I was outdoors and running, I felt the same as everyone else. I ran through a lot of setbacks and failure. I ran through bureaucratic hoops and red tape. I ran in obscurity when all I earned was the minimum wage. I ran at the World Championships in Seville, and at the Sydney 2000 Olympics where I finished eighth in the 1500m. But through it all, I hope I've run for the right reasons: to value effort for its own sake, and to prove that impairment does not preclude excellence.'

'This was a last hurrah ... This was the last chance to fulfil our dreams'

Jason Gardener, member of Britain's Olympic gold medal winning 4x100m Relay team in 2004.

6

UNEXPECTED DRAMA

Munich 1972: War on the Floor

Seoul 1988: The Fastest Loser in the World

Athens 2004: 'Gold, I think'

▲ **14** London 1908: Dorando Pietri, who was disqualified from the Marathon, is presented with a silver trophy by Queen Alexandra as consolation. 'This Cup is balm to my soul,' said the Italian. 'I shall treasure it to the end of my life.'

◀ **15** Munich 1972: Dwight Jones of the USA and Alex Belov of the Soviet Union tip off at the start of the 'War on the Floor' in the Basketball gold medal match. Belov scored to give the Soviet Union a historic and highly controversial victory in the final seconds.

▲ **16** Berlin 1936: the famous photograph of Luz Long and Jesse Owens whose friendship, forged at the 1936 Games, became a powerful symbol of sport's healing powers.

▼ **17** Sydney 2000: Marla Runyan, certified blind and the first Paralympic champion to run in an Olympic Games, leads the field in the semi-final of the 1500m.

▲ **18** Athens 2004: Mark Lewis-Francis flies to victory in the 4x100m Relay. Maurice Greene of the USA, 1/100th of a second behind is out of shot on the left.

▼ **19** The triumphant British 4x100m Relay quartet of (from left) Marlon Devonish, Mark Lewis-Francis, Darren Campbell and Jason Gardener.

▲ **20** Sydney 2000: Dreamtime –
Cathy Freeman contemplates the
enormity of her achievement in
winning the 400m on a star-studded
night in Stadium Australia.

▲ **21** Mexico 1968: David Hemery, the Englishman trained in America, annihilates the field in the 400m Hurdles. His was arguably the greatest performance by a British track athlete at any Olympic Games.

▼ **22** Athens 2004: Paralympic legend Tanni Grey-Thompson celebrates her 10th gold medal, this time in the 100m. Her 11th and last Paralympic gold came in the 400m a few days later.

▲ **23** Rome 1960: The barefooted Ethiopian, Abebe Bikila, leads the Marathon through the streets of the Eternal City. A 28-year-old international novice, his victory on the Appian Way was to herald a new era of African dominance in distance running.

▶ **24** Beijing 2008: The cool runner, Usain Bolt of Jamaica –100m and 200m champion and arch showman of the Olympic Games.

War on the Floor

Munich 1972
Brendan Gallagher

The longest three seconds of in the history of the Games

There has never been a Basketball match quite like it. Could any finish to a major sporting event match the Munich 1972 Olympic Basketball Final between the USA and the USSR? Somehow, early in the morning on the final day of competition in Munich, events at the Rudi-Sedlmayer-Halle seemed to sum up an ill-starred Games. Quickly labelled by the media as the 'War on the Floor', the game was always much more than just the latest man-ifestation of Cold War politics transposed into a sporting arena. This was a match and a sporting moment with a life of its own.

On that frenzied Saturday night in Munich, the USA, undefeated in Olympic Basketball history, were looking for their 63rd consecutive victory in a run that started at the Berlin 1936 Games. They were trailing 49-48 when Doug Collins was fouled and almost knocked out with three seconds left. The first question that begs an answer therefore is why was the game so close? Why weren't the USA home and hosed as they always were by this stage of a game?

The amateur regulations of the day dictated that the

USA was only able to send their top college players to the Games, before they were drafted into the moneymaking machine that is the NBA. In previous years that had not been a problem; the vast arsenal of world-class talent emerging from their main centres of learning had always proved more than sufficient to ensure American supremacy. Now, however, the dynamic was changing and fast. The USSR and Eastern bloc nations, such as the former Yugoslavia, were improving rapidly as the states threw money and facilities at sport.

There was one other problem facing the United States, one that had not previously threatened their domination on the court. As European basketball expanded and developed, the divide between the American game and the European game began to widen. The NBA was not the all-powerful, commercial, machine it is now, but the American way of basketball, even in college – which tended to elevate individual skill over teamwork and speed over height – was increasingly at odds with the slower, more physical, team-oriented, game of the Europeans. It wasn't just subtly different rules on different sides of the Atlantic: this was a matter of style. When the Olympic competition in Munich began, a deeper question was being asked about the future of the sport worldwide. Which game do we want the world to play, the American game or the European game?

So this match was always going to be closer than history suggested. Revisionists may say that it wasn't a particularly vintage college crop in the USA, but nine of the USA's 12-man squad went on to enjoy considerable NBA careers. The USA might not have boasted a stellar line-up, but they were highly skilled. In reality, the match was so close because the USSR had, almost unnoticed, raised their game to new levels. The Soviet Empire was able to incorporate the best players from places such as Lithuania and Latvia – both former European Basketball champions before being annexed by the USSR – while Belarus and Ukraine were also strong basketball nations in their own right.

The USA had enjoyed their normal trouble-free progress to the Final, winning all their seven games and thrashing most sides with embarrassing ease. Only Brazil put up a decent fight before losing 61-54. The USA dispatched Italy 68-38 to secure their place in the final while the Soviet Union, also unbeaten in their seven pool matches, had to work much harder before defeating Cuba 67-61.

At the final, the tension was heightened by the still vivid memory of the Munich massacre just three days earlier. The pre-game mood was emotional and unpredictable. Unaccountably, the USA changed their quick-tempo playing style for something much more cagey and tactical. That has never been fully explained and took out of play their most powerful weapon, the sheer athleticism and speed of their players. In another strange call, coach Hank Iba also chose to use Bobby Jones, their best defender, for only five minutes of the game. Their shooting meanwhile was ragged, while in contrast the USSR's outstanding Siberian, Sergei Belov, often touted as Europe's finest ever player, was in trenchant form, contributing 20 points in an unusually low-scoring game. If the match had ended four minutes from time with the USA eight points behind, there would have been no controversy. The USA had blown it and the USSR were good value for a famous win. Instead the Americans, with public ignominy and disgrace awaiting them back home, somehow dragged themselves back into the game.

With three seconds left, USSR led by one point but a groggy Doug Collins had appeared to knock himself out on the basket stanchion as he was fouled by Zurab Sakandelidze, the tough Georgian from Tbilisi. For a moment, it looked as though the American would have to come off. However, Hank Iba badly wanted Collins, one of the few players on his team to rise to the challenge that day, to stay and take the shots. For once in the match, Iba made exactly the right call.

Collins, still shaken, landed the first free throw without the ball touching the rim to level the scores and then the second for good measure. The score was 50-49 USA, the first time the defending Olympic champions had led all game. Three seconds left. It had to be yet another gold medal for the USA, surely?

Watch, and more importantly listen, to the match video and you will hear a timekeeper's horn go off as Collins launches his second shot. The USSR tried to call a time-out before the final three seconds of the game. Too late. Under the regulations of the tournament, the timeout should have been called and confirmed before Collins attempted his second, seemingly decisive, shot. In any case, nobody on the court heard the horn. The referee, Renato Righetto from Brazil, was unmoved and none of the Soviet or American players reacted. As the second Collins free throw swished through the net, the USA adopted their defensive formation and the USSR clumsily restarted with an attack going nowhere down the right-hand side of the court.

With just one second left, however, Righetto noticed a scuffle by the timekeepers' bench and the USSR's assistant coach, Sergei Bashkin, charged onto the court to call an official timeout. Tempers flared as Bashkin and head coach, Vladimir Kondrashin, then claimed they had called the timeout straight after the foul on Collins, although nobody on the court, players or officials, seemed aware of it.

The USSR argued that their attempt to call a timeout had been thwarted by the language barrier. They spoke poor English, the referee was a Portuguese-speaking Brazilian and the timekeepers German, but the onus when calling a timeout is always on the coaches. Missing a timeout at any level of the game is not unusual. Righetto's decision was 'no timeout'. The Americans were arguing that Bashkin should be called for a technical foul for trespassing on the court, which he was. But by now a much-feared British administrator was descending from his VIP seat in the stand to make a crucial intervention. Renato William Jones was checking in.

William Jones was a patron of the Amateur Basketball Association of England and the long-serving Secretary General of FIBA, the world governing body of the sport. The Italian-born son of a Scottish father who was brought up in Germany, Switzerland and the USA, William Jones was nonetheless a British national and passport holder throughout his life and a hugely influential figure within the game. Rightly or wrongly, FIBA were often seen as being European-orientated and involved in a power battle with the NBA. Being British – complete non-entities in world and Olympic Basketball – William Jones' political stance was that of a neutral, but his powerbase was mainly European. He was certainly seen as a champion of the European game.

William Jones was an accomplished linguist and, with his view from the stands, was possibly able to assess what had happened more quickly and more accurately than most. However he had no official function at the game.

His assessment was that the Soviets had indeed wanted to call a timeout from the start and that, through no fault of their own, the mechanisms in place had failed them. His call was that the game was to be restarted with three seconds left on the clock. He made the point by imperiously raising three fingers at everybody. Referee Righetto strongly disagreed – he insisted that it should still be one second – and subsequently refused to sign the official scoresheet, insisting that the conclusion of the game had been 'irregular', the one thing with which no one involved in the match has ever disagreed.

From chaos the incident now descended into sheer farce. William Jones had unilaterally declared three seconds on the clock and Righetto, although disagreeing strongly, had accepted that he had no option but to officiate along those lines. What exactly to you do when the head of the world governing body marches onto your court and starts throwing his weight around?

The two sides lined up again but unknown to them the single match clock was now, nonsensically, showing 50 seconds. Righetto restarted the game and after just one second with the USSR again going nowhere, the timekeepers realised that the clock was malfunctioning and blew their horn again. The crowd and the joyous Americans thought the game was over and began to celebrate wildly. Up in the stands veteran USA broadcaster Frank Gifford, an NFL legend in his playing days but calling the game for ABC, admitted that he, for one, had absolutely no idea what was going on. He spoke for millions worldwide.

By now the USA assistant coach, Don Haskins, wanted to take the team off the court, but Iba, the head coach, knew only too well that such a move would leave the USA open to a Soviet appeal and the potential forfeit of the gold medal. No matter how much he disagreed with what was going on, at least this way the match could be decided on court. Or as he famously put it, 'I don't want to lose this game later tonight sitting on my butt.' More argument and debate followed, but eventually the game restarted, for the third time, with three seconds on the clock. The Americans were seething but it was not the time to argue or lament. The USA needed to concentrate on seeing out those three seconds.

And then another very strange thing happened. When the game had restarted for the second time big Tom McMillen – who later enjoyed a fine 10-year NBA career and also became a US Congressman – had successfully pressurised Ivan Edeshko and forced him to throw a hurried and ineffectual pass into the backcourt. Now, as the teams lined up for the third restart, Bulgarian official Artenik Arabadjian clearly motioned the 2.11m McMillen to back away – despite the fact that the American was perfectly within his rights to pressurise Edeshko again. Aware how volatile the game had become and how twitchy the officials seemed, and fearful of being penalised if he failed to comply, McMillen reluctantly did as he was told. It was a key moment. Edeshko now had the space to make a superb full court pass to Alexander Belov under the American basket. Arabadjian later denied point blank that he had made any gesture to McMillen, but the video evidence is there for everybody to study.

Still more drama. Belov was being marked by two defenders, Kevin Joyce and Jim Forbes, but both mistimed their challenges and landed off balance. Indeed Joyce's momentum took him right out of play. Belov, on landing with the ball in his hands, had the simplest of lay-ups to win the game. Uproar ensued. Belov sprinted down the court, hands aloft, to join a celebratory scrum of Soviet players and officials. Referee Righetto remained extremely unhappy with the way the game had been taken out of his hands at the end, and the USA immediately lodged an official protest. William Jones, under massive pressure from the Americans, finally decreed that a five-man committee, chaired by Hungary's Ferenc Hepp, should rule on the matter. Poland and Cuba, unsurprisingly, voted for the USSR while Italy and Puerto Rico voted firmly for the USA. Hepp cast the deciding vote in favour of the Soviet Union. That the Soviet bloc nations had potential influence over three of the five committee members was another questionable aspect of the proceedings.

Later that day, at the Victory Ceremony, Olympic officials waited in vain for the Americans to take their place on the podium. The USA team wasn't even in the building. The squad have subsequently taken a collective majority decision not to accept the medals, which remain locked in a vault at the IOC headquarters in Lausanne. Some, like massive centre Tommy Burleson, who didn't get to play in the final but appeared in the pool games, want to relent. He would love a silver medal to pass on to his family to acknowledge the fact that he was an Olympian and that he represented his country in Munich. But the IOC takes the view that either all of the USA team receive their medals or none of them do, so the hard-line approach of the majority prevails.

That something fundamentally unsound occurred that night in Munich would seem beyond doubt. The evidence can be found in the radical changes Basketball – in the NBA and the Olympic Games – quickly introduced to prevent a repeat of the chaos. Major changes to the procedure for calling timeouts were introduced, as well as to the game clocks that recorded to 10ths of a second in the final minute and were to be visible on three sides to players and coaches. There is now a duplicate clock in action at all times and most recently TV replays have been used on site to settle any disputes.

But the rancour continues. The organisers of the 1984 Olympic Games in Los Angeles tried to arrange a dinner for the 12 US players to present them with their medals, but none were willing to attend. In 2002, the respected McMillen formally requested that the IOC revisit the entire incident, quoting two main lines of appeal: a blatant abuse of authority by William Jones and the partisan make-up of the appeal committee. 'If the referees had just made bad judgement calls we would have no case but clearly our game was victimised by manipulation,' argued McMillen cogently. The IOC declined to reconsider the matter then, but 2012 will be the 40th anniversary of the Munich Games and the pressure will surely mount again.

Those three seconds are not over yet; the clock is still counting.

The Fastest Loser in the World

Seoul 1988

Tom Knight

*Ben Johnson's dramatic fall from grace shocked the world,
but helped to change attitudes*

It was clear that Ben Johnson was going to win because of
the unassailable lead he held with the race three-quarters
over. Yet when he crossed the line, his right arm raised,
his forefinger jabbing skywards and glancing sideways
at the vanquished Carl Lewis, his defiant gestures proved
the trigger for a crescendo of noise that greeted this most
astonishing of Olympic triumphs.

By the time Johnson had come to a standstill – and
it could only have been a second or two later – the
100,000-strong crowd squealed with excitement as everyone in the Olympic Stadium noticed the digital reading on
the trackside clock. Not only had Johnson won the gold
medal in emphatic fashion, he had also lowered his own
world record to 9.79 seconds and taken the event, as well
as his own career, into a dimension no one had thought
possible. This was uncharted territory. Just how uncharted
was to become apparent two days later.

For now, though, Johnson had proved himself the best
and fastest sprinter in the world. A US television commentator declared, 'The waiting is over. The questions have all

been answered.' History was to prove him horribly wrong.

It was the first time since Jim Hines, 20 years earlier, that the Olympic champion had also broken the world record, and the startling statistics did not end there. For the first time in the 100m, four men – including Britain's Linford Christie with a European record in third – had run inside the magical 10-second mark and four of the eight finalists had run quicker than they ever had done before. More important than any of the statistics, however, was the manner of Johnson's win because this had always been more than just a race. The men's 100m Final in Seoul 1988 was the face-off, the showdown, akin to a heavyweight contest between two men, in Johnson and Lewis, who didn't like each other.

Johnson had not just beaten Lewis; in athletics terms, he had annihilated him, catapulted from his blocks and run away with the race the whole world had waited 12 months to see. Lewis, the master of the late surge, could not even get close and Johnson's pointing finger let everyone know that he was number one and ready to relish every nanosecond of the moment. As the result lit up the giant Stadium screen, delirium reigned on and off the track. It was hard to know where to look first. As Johnson lapped up the applause and posed for the phalanx of photographers at the end of the straight, Lewis scampered up behind him and tried twice to grab the champion's attention before the pair exchanged a clumsy and token handshake. Visibly shaken by the nature of his defeat, Lewis made a hasty exit, pausing briefly to talk to a US TV crew while Johnson was joined by his teammate, the seventh-placed Desai Williams, before jogging round what became only a half-lap of honour draped in a Canadian flag. The delirium inside the Stadium persisted as people of all nationalities attempted to put into words what they had witnessed.

Lucky to have a seat in the vast press box overlooking the finish line, I turned to a colleague and mouthed, 'Amazing.' Actually I used much stronger language. In those moments it seemed the only possible response, and I know others, including experienced journalists in that Stadium, were lost for words. The sheer excitement of what we had just witnessed was almost overwhelming. It was not the most eloquent response for a so-called writer, but it was an emotion repeated around the Stadium. Maybe it was because this was my first Olympic Games that everything appeared so exciting, but I know that others felt the same. This was a race that everyone had wanted to see because of the history between the two main protagonists and, on reflection, it was no surprise that even hard-nosed, been-there-seen-it journalists from around the world had squeezed into every available space in that press box to witness it. They shared seats, they sat two-abreast on the concrete steps between rows, they crouched down in front of barriers and jostled for a view with the hundreds of South Korean volunteers whose job would be to distribute the result only a few minutes later.

The men's 100m, the Blue Riband event of any championships, had lifted the excitement and drama that was promised to a level that has not been equalled since. In Beijing 20 years later, for example, we all knew that Usain Bolt was going to run fast and that the world record could go. So while the apparent ease with which he achieved both was astonishing, the impact of his victory could not match what happened on that sunny afternoon in Seoul.

The shock in the minutes that followed the race lay in the belief that this was not how the men's Olympic 100m

Final was supposed to turn out. The margin of victory was shocking enough because Lewis, the eloquent American and media-savvy defending champion, had come into the Games as favourite while Johnson, the shy, stuttering Canadian, had struggled all season to maintain the form he had shown the previous year when he had taken the world title with a world record in Rome. Johnson, despite later claiming that he knew what he was doing, had even come close to a calamitous exit in his quarter-final race, when he eased up too soon. He was passed by Christie and Dennis Mitchell, only progressing to the semi-finals as a fastest loser.

The world record was something else altogether. In the weeks before the Olympic Games, Johnson had finished third behind Lewis in Zurich, where he could not maintain his speed over the final third of the race and faded. Four days later, he raced in Cologne and again trailed in third, this time behind Calvin Smith and Mitchell, the Americans who finished fourth and fifth in the Olympic final. Lewis' win in Zurich was his first over Johnson for three years. Few questioned his post-race proclamation that, 'The gold medal for the 100m is mine.'

Chastened and panicking with the Olympic Games only five weeks away, Johnson abandoned the European circuit and returned to his home in Toronto. His Olympic year was not going well after hamstring injuries in February and May, and the lost weeks of training were catching up with him. What we saw in Seoul was that Johnson had made up those lost weeks and returned stronger and faster than he had been in Rome in 1987. It was no surprise that the rumours that began in Rome persisted in Seoul.

In Rome, Lewis had talked of 'people in the sport who

were using drugs' while his teammate, Smith, told the BBC that 'there are a lot of things that are unknown'. Rumours were rife. There were never any names mentioned, of course, but, in those far off times, mutterings about drug taking were not new. You only had to look around the sport to see why suspicion was the norm. After all, this was still a time when, for the majority of athletes, drug testing only happened at competitions. Today's sophisticated system of extensive, unannounced, out-of-season testing was still to be introduced.

Britain's Steve Cram, whose own failure to win anything at 800m or 1500m was disappointing, remembers complaining to the authorities about the inefficiency of the drug testing at grand prix meetings. He said, 'Drug testing was poor then and we accepted that there were a whole bunch of people from several countries who were not playing by the same rules as the rest of us. But it was normality. We didn't see drug testing as something that would catch people.'

Those who came into contact with Johnson in the days before the Athletics programme began had more than enough evidence to give substance to the gossip. Professor Arne Ljungqvist, the distinguished member of the International Olympic Committee and renowned anti-doping campaigner, was on the then IOC's Medical Commission and in charge of drug testing at the Olympic Stadium. He said: 'There was, of course, much speculation about Ben Johnson going into those Games and I had met him for the first time a few days before at an IAAF reception. I remember looking into his yellow eyes, a sign of liver damage caused by drug abuse so, of course, it was good to be mentally prepared for what followed.'

I saw those yellow eyes too. They stared at me through

the windows of a limousine as Johnson was ferried from the Stadium to his hotel in the hours after his victory. As the car passed slowly through a throng of journalists, athletes and officials, I looked into the back seat to see Johnson staring out. The memory can play tricks after more than 20 years, but that particular image of Johnson stayed with me. He looked lost, somehow out of place and diminished by the vastness of the car interior, and I remember thinking that he didn't look like a man who had just won the biggest prize in sport.

Such was the difference between then and now that one British journalist remembers how little discussion there was about drugs after the race. He said: 'There was never any great debate about doping after that race. We just assumed they were all doing it and that they were so good at it, they wouldn't get caught in an Olympic final – and certainly not Ben Johnson.'

Johnson was the last of the medallists to reach the post-race press conference, behind the Stadium in a giant marquee because of the time it had taken him to produce a urine sample. By then, he had already received a congratulatory phone call from Brian Mulroney, the Prime Minister of Canada, and spoken to the BBC's Kevin Cosgrove, who asked Johnson what was more valuable, the world record or a gold medal? Johnson replied, 'The gold medal because it's something no one can take away from you.'

That was Saturday 24 September. By the early hours of 25 September, analysis of Johnson's urine had shown traces of stanozolol, a banned anabolic steroid. When the positive result was confirmed later that day and an appeal by the sprinter was turned down by the IOC's Medical Commission, his fate was sealed. Later, in his hotel room,

Johnson calmly handed back the gold medal with its tri-colour ribbon to Carol Anne Letheren, the Canadian team's Chef de Mission, and plans were made for a hasty departure from Seoul. By the time the IOC gathered the media to confirm Johnson's positive test and disqualifi-cation, he had already been bundled by police through hordes of photographers and camera crews at the airport to catch a flight home.

Canada, which had celebrated Johnson's gold medal and world record, went into meltdown, with opinion divided between those who condemned him for bringing shame to the country and others who clung to the sprint-er's own mantra that he had never knowingly 'taken ille-gal drugs nor have had illegal drugs administered to me'. Back in Seoul, the Olympic Games were overtaken by the debate over doping, which continued to be a live concern.

Johnson was not the only athlete to be expelled from the Games after testing positive; two Bulgarian Weightlifters and Britain's Judo player, Kerrith Brown, also lost medals. But he was the biggest name at Seoul 1988 and the scandal surrounding his drug taking would have ramifications far into the future. An eight-month inquiry into the affair in Canada under Charles Dubin, the Chief Justice of Ontario, unpicked all the rumours, gossip, myths and lies surrounding Johnson's downfall.

As the last of Canada's sense of denial faded in the face of the evidence, the Dubin Inquiry heard taped tele-phone conversations about Johnson's drug regime between his coach, Charlie Francis, and Jamie Astaphan, the St Kitts-based doctor who admitted injecting the sprinter up to 60 times in the five years before Seoul. The last to take the stand and speaking under oath, Johnson finally confessed to using performance-enhancing drugs and said that he was 'ashamed'. Francis was banned for life by Athletics Canada while Johnson served a two-year suspension imposed by the IAAF. He did come back to the sport but without success and was banned for life when he tested positive again in 1993.

Yet ultimately the Johnson affair was to prove cathartic. Change was in the air. The revelations about government-sponsored doping in East Germany that followed the fall of the Berlin Wall only served to strengthen the hand of the IAAF and the IOC in the fight against drugs.

Professor Ljungqvist looks back with mixed feelings. 'The Ben Johnson affair turned out to be a turning point in the fight against doping,' he said. 'We were trying to do something about the evil of doping and working in a difficult environment, politically and psychologically. Many organisations were officially applauding what we were doing but, privately, they did not always support us.

'I remember that I had to conduct the IAAF press conference after the IOC had announced Johnson's positive drug test. The President, Primo Nebiolo, usually loved to be in front of the media and when he asked me to join him in his car on the way to the press conference, you can imagine my shock and surprise when he asked me to take his place on this occasion. It was the first time I had been in this position. It made me feel like a president, sitting in front of all those microphones.

'The question I was asked repeatedly then was "Is this not the death of Olympic sport?" I said "No." This was, instead, finally a chance to show the world that this cannot go on. To cheat and make the world feel disappointed like this could not go on. We understood what was going on and this scandal opened people's eyes even though an atmosphere of general disaster prevailed at the time. The atmosphere around our anti-doping programme changed from a headwind to a tailwind. But sport could not handle the fight against doping alone and moves soon emerged to get other authorities involved. This, ultimately, led to the formation of the World Anti-Doping Agency.

'Looking back, in a way, I'm glad that things happened the way they did. It caused temporary harm and I feel sorry for the organisers of those Olympic Games. In hindsight, however, it was good that it happened that way because it generated so much public support for what we were trying to do in the fight against doping.'

'Gold, I think'

Athens 2004
Andrew Longmore

How the British 4x100m Relay team created one of the biggest shocks in Olympic track history

A television screen flickered silently in the corner of the interview room beneath the Olympic Stadium in Athens. Behind a bank of microphones, Kelly Holmes was explaining to the world's press how, at the age of 34, she had come to win double Olympic gold at the Games. Moments earlier Holmes had cruised past the field in the 1500m to bring her own injury-stricken career to a triumphant conclusion, but, after a thousand interviews, exhaustion was tingeing her elation.

On such a night, being in two places at once is one of the prime skills of a sports writer. But there was no chance of anyone trumping a double gold medallist. We had the story. Surely?

On the screen, the British 4x100m Relay squad were preparing to take on the Americans. The gold was as good as gone – the USA had three Olympic champions in their quartet and all four had run under 10 seconds in the 100m trials – but maybe our team could defy the odds and edge a silver. Yet the British squad of Darren Campbell, Marlon Devonish, Jason Gardener and Mark Lewis-Francis had not qualified for any of the individual finals in Athens, and their heart and character had been openly questioned by Colin Jackson and Michael Johnson, two influential voices in the BBC commentary box. Campbell and Johnson had exchanged words when they met by accident only a few nights before and Campbell, a more sensitive soul than he cares to show, was still seething at the indignity.

No, Kelly would still be the main story by morning. The noise of the crowd filtered through to the interview room, announcing the start of the men's Relay. Soundlessly, two athletes flashed across the finishing line, almost inseparable: on the near side the recognisably muscular figure of Maurice Greene, but on the far side? In the royal blue and white? The French? The Italians? The British? No, surely not the British? Behind me, a fellow journalist whispered: 'Did we win silver?' 'No,' I replied, 'gold, I think.'

Upstairs in the press tribune, it was pandemonium. Kelly's story was written, but, for shocking spontaneity, this was better. The first British Relay triumph in a major championships since 1912 and against probably the most powerful American squad in Relay history. The British team had barely reached the final, barely qualified for the whole event, having been ranked 15th out of the 16 teams eligible to run. Their history was littered with dropped batons and internal dissent.

Slowly, we tried to piece together the 38.07 seconds of action. In lane three, the changeovers of the British team – Gardener to Campbell to Devonish and, finally, Lewis-Francis – had been swift and slick; in lane five, the Americans were cocky and unpractised. Their changeovers were rusty and sluggish. When Justin Gatlin hurtled towards Coby Miller at the end of the second leg, Miller couldn't hear the call. He panicked, went too soon and took the baton at a virtual standstill.

Sensing the Americans' distress, Devonish ran a brilliant final bend and gave young Lewis-Francis, a former gold medallist in the World Junior Championships, a precious advantage. A metre, a metre and a half? Lewis-Francis did not stop to look. He just put his head down and flew as if the devil himself was on his tail.

Inch by inch, Greene closed him down and, by the line, just one hundredths of a second separated the two. It was enough. The British four had won and their celebrations were tellingly impromptu. Gardener, Devonish and Lewis-Francis jigged up and down in delight before Campbell too came to share the moment. Up in the stands, the phones were ringing hot back to London as the enormity of the achievement began to sink in. Deadlines were getting close, yet here was another great British triumph.

Jason Gardener still remembers the eerie sense of calm on the coach as the team made its way to the Olympic Stadium for the final. He had never known such an air of confidence before such a coiled-spring event, but it was there in the whole team. In Devonish, the most laid back of the foursome anyway; in Lewis-Francis, the youngest and most vulnerable; Campbell, the elder statesman and usually the most talkative; and in Gardener himself, the technician, the thinker in the team. The tactics had been talked through. The semi-final, in which they had come perilously close to elimination, had been set to one side and the dominance of the Americans analysed and confronted.

Two factors were working in their favour: one was their teamwork and the other was Coby Miller. With the exception of Lewis-Francis, the British team had been running together most of their lives. Gardener and Devonish first met as teenagers and they had developed a close friendship on the way to the top. Gardener and Campbell's relationship was more fractious, but they had mutual respect for each other's ability. Campbell, brash and insecure, was a complex character. He had been tough enough to survive a childhood in Moss Side, one of Manchester's most notorious neighbourhoods, and to have carved out a decent career for himself at the highest level of sprinting, but several times in his career he had become disillusioned with the sport, once disappearing off to the west to play football for Plymouth Argyle reserves, and he never felt fully accepted within the British system. He was 30 at the Athens 2004 Games, and coming to the end of a career that lacked only the crowning glory of Olympic gold. Hurt by the criticism from Michael Johnson that he had faked injury in the individual 100m and 200m, he was more than ready to set the record straight in the Relay. Gardener, too, had been hit by injury after winning gold at the World Indoor Championships that spring and was still running with a fractured wrist when he arrived in the Greek capital. Devonish was just Devonish. And no one knew which Lewis-Francis might turn up.

Long before Athens, the core of the team, augmented by Lewis-Francis, had committed themselves to winning the gold medal in Athens. In practical terms that meant sacrificing some of their individual ambitions for the sake of the team, trying to coordinate complicated schedules. Emotionally it meant committing to a distant but attainable goal. 'For me and Darren, this was a last hurrah,' Gardener recalled. 'This was the last chance to fulfil our dreams.'

The weak link in the seemingly unbreakable American chain was Miller, the only non-Olympic champion in the team. Miller was a considerable sprinter, a sub-10 second 100m runner, but he had not been chosen for any of the individual events and the British knew he would be nervous, anxious not to let his more illustrious team-mates down. Miller, a strong 200m runner, would run the third leg and if the British could exert some pressure on the Americans through the first two legs, there was just a chance that he might crack. The Americans' traditional cockiness masked a lack of practice. Gatlin, Greene and Shawn Crawford had been too busy focussing on individual glory to worry much about the Relay and the more they strutted their stuff, the better the British felt about their own chances.

It did not look promising in the semi-finals. The British had come second and their baton-changing was a fraction off-key. On the track after the race, Gardener gathered the team together and told them to be positive. 'We can win this,' he said. By design, they hurried through the media area barely stopping for the BBC, let alone the written press. 'We didn't want any negative thoughts to come into our minds at all,' said Gardener later. 'So we just said: "We finished second, we're in the final" and off we went.' Slowly, over the next 24 hours, the belief and commitment began to deepen. Yes, their semi-final was not perfect, but they were running well and fast, if they could just sharpen those changeovers. The Americans, who had yet to field their A team, were not convincing either.

On the day of the final, in Gardener's mind at least, that belief had grown into an almost inexplicable certainty. They could win this. Little things were telling him so. In the warm-up area, there were two tracks, one on higher ground than the other. Instinctively, the British warmed up on the top track from where they were able to look down on their American rivals. Gardener stopped

Campbell from bad-mouthing the Americans. No reason to give them any reason to be angry. The Americans were late into the call-room before the race. They were always late. It was part of their psychological strategy, a way of making the other finalists feel inferior. But this time the ploy backfired. The Americans arrived to find the British team being photographed with some of the Greek volunteers, laughing and joking as if out for a Sunday stroll. No one noticed the Americans' entrance, but Gardener was reminded of a strange meeting he'd had the previous day with one of the Greek track officials. 'The British will win, I tell you,' the official had said. 'You are going to beat the Americans.' To this day, Gardener does not know the name of the official, but he would like to thank him for his conviction.

There was one other thing. When he was handed his baton, Britain's baton, it was coloured gold. He sneaked a look at the Nigerians in the next lane, no, they had a blue baton; the Americans' baton was a different colour again. By the time Gardener settled into his blocks to run the anchor leg, he felt an overwhelming sense of destiny. Then he false started.

One more false start and, under new rules, any one of the athletes could be disqualified, so the pressure was not just on Gardener, but the whole field. Once out of the blocks, Gardener concentrated on cutting the corner as tightly as he could and on closing the gap with the Nigerian on his outside. Put the pressure on the Americans, keep the pressure on. He had handed over the baton to Campbell so many times, he knew that Campbell's hand would go up and then down to collect the baton. The British used the push method for the change – hand out, push in – but the timing has to be perfectly choreographed. Gardener to Campbell was *perfect*, Campbell streaked down the back straight, trying to match the giant figure of Gatlin, who exuded power. The change to Devonish was equally slick. But the Americans knew they were in a race now and, when Gatlin hurtled towards Miller, at just the point that the British team and their coaches had planned, they made a decisive mistake.

Setting off from his blocks a fraction of a second too early, Miller had to break his stride to wait for Gatlin. Timing was now awry, with Miller's right hand far too high for Gatlin to make an easy switch. The change was slow and awkward; Miller was swamped by the Nigerian athlete and by Devonish, who had run a stunning bend to sneak through on the inside. Gardener could do nothing but watch from across the track, his line of sight impeded by all the officials. 'I couldn't believe the lead Mark had and I was thinking: "If you lose that…" but I didn't see the finish. All I could see was Mark bouncing up and down,' Gardener recalled. Soon, all four of the squad were bouncing up and down, relishing a spectacular and emotional triumph.

Both Gardener and Campbell called time on their athletics careers before the next Olympic Games in Beijing. Devonish stayed on to compete in Beijing 2008 and helped to guide an inexperienced British quartet to an unlikely bronze in the 4x100m Relay at the 2009 World Championships in Berlin. Lewis-Francis has yet to make the breakthrough into the very top rank, but is still competing hard. They have never had a reunion to remember their victory, nor ever truly stopped to celebrate the moment or catch each other's memories. One day, maybe. What matters is that, for 38.07 seconds on a warm night in Athens, they were the fastest team in the world.

'It had to be a world record because I knew that's what it would take to win … if I ran my perfect race I could finish ahead of everyone'

David Hemery, Olympic 400m Hurdles champion at the 1968 Olympic Games.

7
SIX OF THE BEST

The Golden Arrow

Rome 1960
Kate Battersby

How the remarkable Margaret Maughan won Britain's first Paralympic gold medal

Sporting milestones have a habit of announcing their achievements with fanfares. But sometimes history in the making is whispered, not shouted. Now and then, landmark moments steal by all but unobserved, clouded in confusion, revealed only later.

Monday 19 September 1960 was a long, hot day in Rome. Margaret Maughan, a 32-year-old domestic science teacher, was representing Britain on the first day of the ninth International Stoke Mandeville Games, just 19 months after a car accident rendered her a T11 paraplegic.

'My event was bewildering,' recalls Maughan of the Columbia Round Open in the Archery. 'There were rows and rows of us from different competitive classes. The way they kept track of the scores was very complicated and we couldn't follow it. We finished our competition and the scorers just went away, so we didn't have any idea how we'd done. The day just went by, and we went off to support others on the team. It seemed quite natural.'

It was mid-evening, and the British competitors had already gone through the arduous business of being put on their team coach to go back to their accommodation, before the matter was raised again.

'Someone said: "Where's Margaret Maughan? She's got to come and get a medal." But I still had no idea what colour. It was beginning to get dark now. So I was taken off the coach and we were wheeled up the ramp to go on to the podium, and that was when I was told I had won the gold. Hardly anyone was there to see. It was just bewildering, to be honest. But it was emotional. I had a frog in my throat listening to the national anthem.'

It would be another 24 years before the International Olympic Committee approved the term 'Paralympic', and the ninth International Stoke Mandeville Games was recognised as having been the first Summer Paralympic Games. Margaret Maughan was 56 by the time she was pronounced as having become Britain's first ever Paralympic gold medal winner a generation previously. Yet even now she finds it difficult to take pride in something achieved, as she sees it, by an accident of scheduling.

'I feel a fraud,' she says frankly, sitting at her kitchen table. 'There were so many others who got on and did interesting things too. I feel they're being left out. I just represent them. I feel guilty. I don't like pushing myself forward.'

Yet if anything is clear talking to Maughan it is that she must always have been a remarkable woman, such was her spirit of enterprise. Her childhood, however, was conventional. She was born in a Lancashire village in June 1928, one of four children of a miner turned market gardener. It was a happy, Methodist upbringing.

'Everything we did went on around the village chapel,' remembers Maughan. 'I wasn't sporty at all as a child. I wasn't interested. I didn't like sport at school. I was a bit overweight and wasn't good at hockey or any of those things. But later in my 20s I did play quite a bit of badminton and tennis, although only on a social level.'

After spending three years working as a domestic science teacher at a school in Jamaica, Maughan embarked on what was planned to be a similar term in the former Nyasaland, now Malawi. Judging by the smile spreading over her still-unlined features, those were exciting times.

'It was a big adventure in those days. I had itchy feet and wasn't meeting many people. As a schoolteacher you tended to be in rather a closed environment. I wasn't daunted, although I don't know how I did it as I was a real village girl. I'd never been to London or anything when I went to college, which was in Edinburgh. But travel didn't faze me and I wanted to do it. I was hoping I would be in Africa for several years, maybe get married and have a family there.'

However her life as she had known it changed in one February night in 1959, when she was 30. She tends not to speak of it readily, describing it merely as 'the past', which she simply doesn't think about. But she still recalls what happened with perfect clarity.

'Nyasaland was a social kind of place, like so many British ex-colonies. I was with a friend on my way to a party. He was driving. It was a Volkswagen Beetle – without seatbelts, of course. We were going too fast. The roads were very poor although ironically we were on the only bit of tarmac road in that part of Malawi. The car lost control and rolled over and over, landing upside down in the scrubland bush at the side of the road.

'I knew something had happened because I couldn't move. My friend was perfectly all right. He just got out of the car, but he couldn't get me out. I was very frightened. It was very, very painful. The first people to arrive were two truck drivers and I refused to let them touch me because I knew it was going to hurt so much.'

She was taken to a local hospital, and then flown to a larger facility in Blantyre, now the second largest city in Malawi. Days later a surgeon was flown in from South Africa to operate, and it was during this procedure – a laminectomy – that it was discovered her spinal cord was severed at the eleventh thoracic bone (hence T11).

'So I was paralysed, but they didn't tell me that. I can remember one nurse saying, "Oh, you'll be all right." I didn't ask if I would be able to walk again. Weird, isn't it? But I couldn't move at all, so I suppose I knew.'

Maughan was there for two months before she was told she was to be flown back to Britain, and the 'very famous' Stoke Mandeville hospital, which she had never heard of. On arrival she found it bewildering.

'There were these big, long wards with 20 or 30 beds. I remember someone in an iron lung, and a great hush when the iron lung went off and everyone knew that person had died. A lovely consultant came and saw me straight away. He put it fairly plainly that I wouldn't ever be able walk again and that was that. I didn't burst into tears. I wasn't a crying sort of person.'

But she admits she was crying one afternoon when 'this little man' arrived at her bedside. She did not know it then, but he was Ludwig Guttmann, a neurosurgeon now considered the founder of the Paralympic Games.

'You knew immediately by his bearing that he was someone important. He told me I had to start getting on with things and not feel sorry for myself, and that meeting had a great effect on me. It was something I bore in mind always.'

It was June, four months after the accident, before she

got out of bed and into a wheelchair. Archery, which she had never tried before, was part of patient rehabilitation because it helped balance and posture – and it was immediately clear that Maughan was good at it.

'I liked it,' she smiles. 'I won competitions. It made me feel good.'

She was in Stoke Mandeville for almost a year and counts herself lucky that her teaching salary was paid in full throughout that time. On release she lived at her parents' house in Lancashire and joined the local archery club. 'They were so kind to me. They had no other disabled members, of course. They hadn't really seen many people like me.'

That June she took part in the National Stoke Mandeville Games, and was 'amazed' to receive a letter saying she had been selected for that September's International Games in Rome. Travel was a complicated business.

'We needed a lot of male escorts to lift each of us out of our wheelchairs into a coach, or out of a coach, and then they had to sort through the labelled wheelchairs to find which was yours. To get on the plane to Rome, four of us at a time were put on the forklift platform to get to the door of the plane, and then each of us would be lifted out of the chair, put in a seat and each wheelchair put in the hold. You can imagine it all took ages.' Nor was the accommodation in Rome quite what was required.

'It was hopelessly unsuitable. Nothing was on the ground floor. The buildings were all on stilts. The Italians called the army in who were on duty all day and night. They worked in teams, two on each half landing, to carry us up and then carry our wheelchairs up, and then down again. We were very grateful.'

Although most famous for her triumph in the Archery,

Maughan won a second gold medal in Rome 1960. It came in the women's Backstroke Complete Class 5, in the Olympic pool where Anita Lonsbrough had won gold for Britain weeks before in the 200m Breaststroke.

However, Maughan took little delight in her own victory. 'That was awful. I wasn't a great swimmer. It was the last day. I had hardly ever swum 50m in my whole life. I got changed and sat and waited, and became clear that I was the only person entered in that race, and they were going to call it off. But on the team leaderboard it was very tight between the Italians and British and I did it to get the extra points for that. I didn't enjoy it. I'm not proud of that gold medal.'

By now Maughan found that competitive fever flowed in her blood and she was hugely let down not to be selected for the 1964 International Games.

By 1968 she was competing at a far more senior level and found the going tougher, finishing fourth and fifth in two classes of Archery. Four years later in Heidelberg she was sixth in her Archery class, but won gold in 'Dartchery – a fun thing invented for us … Archery on a target laid out like a dartboard'. In 1976 the Toronto Games were open for the first time to many disabilities, and Maughan took another silver in the Dartchery, along with silver in the Lawn Bowls. All this time between Paralympic Games she was competing in the Commonwealth Games For The Paralysed, where she won so many golds in Archery and Table Tennis that she literally lost count. But after Toronto, the passing years prompted her to give up Archery.

'I didn't like taking part if I wasn't going to win. I know the Olympic Creed is about the taking part, not the winning, but that wasn't for me. I wasn't getting good scores and I didn't like that. I wanted to win.'

Arnhem 1980 was her last Paralympic Games, where she won her final gold, in the Lawn Bowls. Her Paralympic career had spanned 20 years. In the Rome 1960 Games, 400 competitors from 23 nations took part in 57 events covering eight sports. At Arnhem there were 1,973 competitors from 42 nations with 489 events in 12 sports. And in London 2012 there will be around 4,200 athletes, with 503 events in 20 sports.

'We're all so proud that we were in there at the beginning,' says Maughan. 'Something that started so small has become so huge.'

Then she leans forward in her wheelchair, and confides with a smile, 'Actually, we used the word "Paralympic" right from the beginning. When it acquired wider use, we were a bit jealous; it didn't mean just those in wheelchairs anymore. We were originally "the paras". We were very daring, you know. Life has to be got on with. It's what you make of it, isn't it?'

'Hemery first, the rest nowhere'

Mexico City: 1968
Neil Wilson

The triumph of a very modest Englishman

'Hemery leads … It's Hemery, Great Britain. It's Hemery, Great Britain … And David Hemery's going to take the gold. David Hemery wins for Britain. In second place is Hennige. And who cares who's third? It doesn't matter … Hemery won that from start to finish. He killed the rest. He paralysed them.'

David Coleman's commentary on the 400m Hurdles at the Mexico City 1968 Olympics is as memorable to those who stayed up late to watch on BBC television as the race itself. As Hemery himself has said since, I've tried watching it without the commentary. It's colourless.' How Coleman described it was as perfectly measured as Hemery's performance, a moment as seminal for sports broadcasting as the athlete's performance was for the event of 400m Hurdles.

Each evening for two weeks before the race, Hemery had walked around the Estadio Olímpico visualising himself running. He did it for each of the eight lanes because he did not know which he would draw, and at the end he always won in a world record time. 'It had to be a world record because I knew that's what it would take to win,' he said. 'When I visualised the race in my head, it was in the greatest sensory detail. Even my heart-rate and breathing-rate would rise. I thought that if I ran my perfect race I could finish ahead of everyone.'

Hemery and his British teammate, John Sherwood, the man from Sheffield who came third and Coleman thought didn't matter, were the slowest in the field of eight going into the final. Sherwood had set, and Hemery equalled, the British record at 49.3 seconds in their semi-finals. All three in the US team had run faster in their Olympic trials!

Yet the final on 15 October 1968 was no race at all on a night when lightning lit the skies. Hemery, drawn in lane six, had decided to go fast from the start because he feared the American Ron Whitney's fast finish. Whitney was one lane outside him, in his sights.

Hemery was first to rise to hurdle one, his long legs flicking over the 3ft hurdles as though he was running a flat race, a trotting horse as he once described his leg action. At halfway he had wheeled in Whitney's stagger and taken a lead of 6m, arriving at the 200m mark in a time of 23.0, seven-tenths of a second faster than the British record for the Hurdles distance.

It is the common wisdom of coaches that a reckless first half is paid for in spades in the straight as the legs drown in lactic acid, but Hemery's lead only grew. He increased his strides between the barriers from 13 to 15 around the long final curve, and when he crossed the line in 48.12 seconds he was 7m and nine-tenths of a second ahead of Gerhard Hennige of West Germany. Hemery first, rest nowhere, as one British newspaper told it.

It was the greatest winning margin since the 1924 Olympic Games, a world record by seven-tenths of a second, and yet Hemery admitted later that he was unsure of victory until a BBC television crew came running towards him. 'I'd have been very disappointed if I hadn't won,' said Hemery.

The perfect ending to his day came when he was presented with gold by the Marquis of Exeter, an International Olympic Committee member and President of the International Amateur Athletic Federation who, as David Burghley, won the event at the Amsterdam 1928 Games (the last Briton to do so). 'I'd have been very disappointed if I hadn't won,' observed Hemery again.

That was not immodesty. Of that, Hemery was incapable. He was, as Sir Arthur Gold – who was to become the President of the European Athletic Association – put it, quoting a line from Chaucer, 'A verray parfit gentil knight.' Or as an American reporter described, 'The kind of British guy you only ever see in the movies.'

Hemery's confidence lay in his knowledge of all he had done to arrive at that point of perfection, the training of his body and the hardening of his mind to running the sort of time he correctly calculated would be too fast for his rivals.

Tall at 1.87m, fair-haired and classically Edwardian in appearance, he cut a Corinthian figure in all things, charming, polite and diffident of manner. It was hard to believe when meeting him, but behind that facade was a man who would drive himself beyond normal human limits to achieve, who had a competitive streak honed by seven years spent in the United States where his father was a financial consultant.

He was fortunate to have innate speed-endurance. He ran a lap of an English 440-yard track at the age of 11 in 68.7 second, and he was well taught as a hurdler by a Harrow schoolmaster, Fred Housden. He won the AAA and Commonwealth Games 110m Hurdles titles by the age of 21, an event he put to one side because he never thought much of himself as a sprinter.

Hemery returned to the United States to study for a degree at the University of Boston, a decision that was to prove crucial to his development when he decided he had more chance of international success at 400m Hurdles. The coach at Boston, Billy Smith, was a driver of men, demanding the most and exacting the best. Fate had given him the perfect pupil.

The 400m Hurdles was described in a book by a noted American coach, Dean B. Cromwell, as 'clearly invented with homicidal intent'. One lap of the track flat out, with the rhythm constantly broken by 10 barriers almost a metre in height. After a runner has gone 300m fatigue kicks in and, if he lands without the body exactly over the foot, he will stagger, wasting more precious energy. The energy output is more like sprinting 800m.

The hills around Boston and the sand dunes on the Massachusetts coast became Hemery's playground. His programme demanded runs up 30m-high dunes 35 times. No account was given to weather. Once, when heavy snow had fallen, Hemery recalled, Smith swept a single lane of the university track so he could train. 'Out there lays the road to Mexico,' he would say.

Before the Mexico City 1968 Games, Hemery had completed 59 of the 60 weeks of unremitting training that Smith's programme demanded. He missed one week because of influenza. Yet in 1967 he had raced only once – a 110m Hurdles – because of a badly torn hamstring, so he was competitively rusty coming into Olympic year.

To his rivals, he was not a factor in their calculations at the start of the 1968 season. He had never run faster than 51.8 seconds, almost three seconds off the world record, and it was that time he equalled in his first race of the summer, a university competition in Boston. From that point, though, his improvement was continual and rapid. He won the US National Collegiate title, beating Geoff Vanderstock who was to break the world record in the US Olympic trials, and on his return to Britain he ran a personal best of 49.6.

Hemery had two disadvantages as a Hurdler, the first you would think fundamental. He is short-sighted. He sees at 20m what those with normal vision see at 200m. He thought at the time of his running career that it improved his hearing, enabling him to hear how far others were ahead or behind him, but when you are running flat out into a hard wooden barrier poor sight is not a virtue.

A second drawback was Hemery's inability to hurdle off his left foot. So when fatigue shortened his stride after five flights of hurdles, he could not put in just an extra stride to compensate. It had to be two so he would be flying off his right foot. At a point where others might be slowing, he had to accelerate to accommodate two more shorter strides.

He had, though, one enormous advantage as an athlete. His mind. He has earned his living by talking and writing about sport. His PhD thesis, which became a book *The Pursuit of Sports Excellence*, illuminates the mental aspect. 'Fred Housden taught me how to hurdle, Billy Smith to work and I added the third component which is what's going on in the mind,' he said.

Competition had fascinated him from his earliest memory. He remembers competing against himself, how long he could hold his breath, how many jumps he could make on a pogo stick, anything to test himself. An Olympic

Games was just the ultimate challenge, 'the last piece in the jigsaw', as he described winning.

It was the reason he quit the 400m Hurdles as an event the moment he won his Olympic gold. He had challenged himself. It was no longer a challenge. He decided to test himself at athletics' ultimate challenge, the Decathlon. He was not a huge success. He was not a sprinter by nature, and that is fundamental to the decathlete, and his best score of 6,893 points, while earning him a place in the British team, was not close to international standard.

Injuries drove him away from that challenge but still he refused to resume in the event in which he was Olympic champion. He returned instead to High Hurdles, won a silver medal at the European Championships in 1969 and successfully defended his Commonwealth title in 1970. By the time he had finished with the event, he had set six British records but again he recognised that he would not be among the contenders at the Olympic Games.

So by the Munich 1972 Games he had decided that it had to be a re-run of the 400m Hurdles if he was to make the team with any chance of success. He returned to Boston to train under Smith, but in truth his heart was never fully in it. He said years later that he ran because he thought he ought to. 'I was there on an "ought" rather than a personal desire to prove myself.'

The mental images he conjured up this time were more negative. He was thinking 'I'll do my best' more than 'I am going to win'. He never steeled himself to win and recalls walking into the Olympic Stadium for the final, digging his nails into his palms and saying: 'For God's sake, wake up.'

His natural talent and work ethic earned him the bronze medal, but the event had been moved on by his superlative performance in Mexico City. A Ugandan, John Akii-Bua, coached by a Welshman, Malcolm Arnold, came out of nowhere to take the gold medal and obliterate the world record that had seemed so untouchable when it was created in the thin air of Mexico City.

Hemery helped the British 4x400m Relay team to a silver medal at the end of those Games, but then looked outside the sport for further challenges. He gained a Certificate of Education at Oxford University and taught at Millfield School in Somerset, a high-achievers' academy. He then moved back to Boston to take an MA in Education at Harvard and coached at his former university.

For many years now he has been enjoying the life of a family man in Wiltshire, running a company giving seminars that use the analogies between sport, business and competition while serving as Deputy Chairman of the British Olympic Association. His motivational talks to corporate leaders and today's hurdlers are hugely respected, but it is for that moment lasting a lot less than one minute in Mexico City 1968 that he will be remembered. It was, and will always remain, one of the greatest performances in an Olympic Games by a Briton, certainly among the most memorable.

Cathy Comes Home

Sydney 2000

Andrew Longmore

On a golden night of athletics, Cathy Freeman ran the race of her life

In the back straight of the Olympic Stadium in Sydney, opposite the main stand, Phillips Idowu was on the runway about to take his fourth attempt in the Triple Jump. This was the young British athlete's first major championships and he'd already ignored the advice of a teammate not to look up when he first entered the Stadium. He had looked up and been overwhelmed by the expectation of 110,000 people. The expectations were not for him, he knew, but the air was crackling, which made a change from the last time he'd competed, in front of a few hundred people on a windswept afternoon in Gateshead.

More than any other athlete, jumpers like to engage with their audience. They clap their hands rhythmically above their head, encouraging the crowd to join in. But just as the flamboyant Idowu was starting his routine, the sound of the starting gun triggered an explosion of noise. Idowu knew what that meant. Cathy Freeman was coming. 'I didn't know the rules so I thought I'd better get going,' Idowu recalled a few days later. 'The noise was so deafening I had to put my fingers in my ears, but I didn't want to be racing Cathy down the back straight, so I just told myself they were cheering for me.'

On the crown of the home bend, the women pole vaulters were also in mid-competition. Stacy Dragila, the favourite for gold, was taking her third attempt at 4.50m. It was a critical jump. She, too, heard Freeman coming and was wondering what to do when the officials halted the competition. So the American paused and watched as Freeman, dressed in her hooded green and gold catsuit, swept by. 'There was so much energy in the air,' Dragila said.

Monday 25 September 2000 will go down as one of the greatest nights of Athletics in Olympic history. 'Every time I turned round,' observed Idowu, 'there was another legend running past me.' One by one, they flew by on their way into the record books. On that night, Michael Johnson won his fourth gold medal, annihilating the field in the 400m with that stiff, upright, running style. Gaby Szabo, the petite Romanian, turned her world records into the grand currency of gold in the 5,000m after an epic duel with Ireland's Sonia O'Sullivan. Ethiopia's Haile Gebrselassie ran one of the greatest races of his life to repel the challenge of the Kenyan, Paul Tergat, over a blistering final lap, becoming only the third man after Emil Zátopek and Lasse Virén to defend his 10,000m Olympic title. For many, however, the warm, sultry night will be remembered for just one waif-like figure and for just one ineradicable image. Cathy Freeman, sitting alone on the track, barefoot, dazed, suspended for a millisecond between past and present, like a dreamer waking from sleep.

Slowly, Freeman arose to greet her new world. With the Australian flag in one hand and the black, red and yellow flag of her Aboriginal people in the other, the new 400m champion did a lap of honour that encompassed every acre of her vast land and every race, colour and creed within it. It was the second time Freeman had lit up the Olympic Stadium. Eleven nights earlier she had stood cold and wet beneath a waterfall, praying that a technical hitch in the lighting of the Olympic Cauldron would not spoil the moment of release for a nation prone just briefly in the days leading up to the 2000 Games to self-doubt. But the gas in the Torch held out just long enough and in one symbolic gesture Freeman, clad in a white catsuit, opened the Millennium Games and illuminated one of the darkest passages in Australian history.

For years before the Games, debate had raged over whether the Australian government should issue an official apology to the Stolen Generation, the thousands of Aboriginal children who had been taken from their homes and forcibly resettled. Freeman's grandmother was one of those children and, though the government did not issue that apology for another eight years, the decision to give an Aboriginal athlete the central role in the most historic tableau in Australia's sporting history was deemed to be a sign of reconciliation. In 1990, at the Commonwealth Games in Auckland, Freeman had become the first Aboriginal to win a gold medal for Australia. Now she was representing her people, all her people, on the biggest sporting stage of all. Not once, but twice.

The video of Freeman's run has become part of the British team's psychological preparation for the London 2012 Games. The subliminal message is quite clear: if you think you've got pressure, watch this. But the way Cathy – or Catherine as she prefers to be called – Freeman tells it, the pressure seemed greater from the outside than from within. Partly, that was due to Freeman's own background, her love of nature and a fatalism that comes from the Bahá'í Faith adopted by her mother, Cecelia. 'I'm very good at detaching myself from what's happening outside,' she said. 'I guess I've always been away with the fairies a bit. Maybe that just comes from being a bush kid, living without the pressure you live with every day in the city. My mother was always telling me I have to concentrate on my spirituality.'

Freeman was brought up in the town of Mackay in northern Queensland. In her autobiography, she recalled a childhood running barefoot in the wasteland, playing in the streams and trying to hide from her own talent. Her stepfather, Bruce Barber, was her first coach, the first to notice that the frailest-looking of the five Freeman children could run like the wind. Freeman won her first gold medal at the age of eight and showed such athletic talent that she won scholarships initially to the Kooralbyn International School, an independent co-educational school south of Brisbane, and then to Fairholme College, another independent school, in Toowoomba in the southeast of Queensland.

By then, she had been taken on by her first professional coach, Mike Danila, a Romanian, and was on the path to national recognition. But there was still a long way to go, for Freeman, for her state and her country. Less than a century earlier, the Queensland Amateur Athletics Association had tried to ban Aboriginal athletes from competing against whites. The reasons for the ban were complex and not fully understood by the officials themselves, but at the heart of it was the plainest sporting fear of all – the fear of defeat. As early as the late nineteenth century Aboriginal sprinters had proved themselves to be devastatingly quick, often much quicker than their white opponents. As well as protecting the 'moral' authority of the average Australian, segregation was a convenient way of protecting the cash prizes that went to the victors at high profile country meetings.

One of the most famous of the late nineteenth-century athletes was Charlie Samuels, an Aboriginal who trained on a diet of 'cigars, tobacco and plenty of sherry' and who reputedly ran the 100 yards in 9.1 seconds in a race at Botany, Sydney, in 1888. Even the *Referee*, one of Australia's first sporting newspapers, had to acknowledge the fact that Samuels was the champion runner of Australia. Samuels fell into a life of crime and penury and died at the age of 49 in a government penal establishment, which only reinforced racial stereotypes. Boxing, Rugby League and Australian Rules Football were the most popular outlets for Aboriginal athletic talent through the twentieth century as social and sporting barriers slowly began to break down. Both Freeman's father and grandfather were renowned Rugby League players. By the time the three Ella brothers, Mark, Glen and Gary, emerged from La Pelouse in New South Wales to represent Australia at Rugby Union, still a game for amateurs, in the 1980s the only stereotype left was the old one (not unknown to the first black footballers in England) about black athletes falling to pieces under pressure.

If any perception of frailty still lingered over Freeman's lithe figure in Sydney, it had evaporated 49.11 seconds of blurred action later. Away with the fairies Freeman might have been, but she was also a ruthless and analytical competitor, a runner who cared far more about winning than about times or records. Coming into the Sydney 2000 Olympic Games, Freeman's winning streak stretched back 46 races. Since taking some time off after winning gold at the World Championships in Athens in

1997, and concentrating solely on the 400m, she had become unbeatable, twice a world champion, blessed with the stamina of a long distance runner, the rhythmic stride of a natural 400m athlete and the finishing kick of a 200m specialist.

The only person who could still touch her was Marie-José Pérec, the 1992 and 1996 Olympic champion. But Pérec had not been in good form and her volatile temperament did not survive the rough and tumble of the first few days in Sydney. Claiming to have been harassed by the Australian press, she turned on her heels and fled the country. Freeman's main rival did not even make the start-line, a matter of delight to the local favourite at the time and a source of regret ever since. Without Pérec, Freeman was virtually unchallenged. All she had to do was run within herself, not be drawn into a race against the clock by the emotions of the moment, and the gold medal was all but around her slender neck.

'It was fear that kept me from going faster,' said Freeman afterwards. 'I forced myself to be practical. I ran one of the most conservative races of my life.' Behind her, at a respectful distance, came Lorraine Graham of Jamaica and Katharine Merry of Britain. Conservative, but smart. Under the guidance of her coach, Peter Fortune, Freeman had made a plan and stuck rigidly to it, always one of the keys to success in Olympic sport. Alone on the track, Freeman might have looked as if she was in the state known in Aboriginal culture as Dreamtime, but her race technique had been focussed, unfussy, flawless.

Much was written at the time about the healing powers of Freeman's victory. Much the same was written about South Africa's win in the 1995 Rugby World Cup when Nelson Mandela donned a Springbok jersey, once a hated symbol of apartheid, and about the cultural significance of the multi-racial France team of Zinedine Zidane, Patrick Vieira and Youri Djorkaeff that won the 1998 FIFAWorld Cup. Ten years on from the Sydney 2000 Games, the Australian Olympic Committee held a dinner at which Freeman was the guest of honour. 'Catherine,' said John Coates, President of the AOC, 'you have become an institution.' The choice of words was apt, as much a source of pride for Freeman as her original gold medal. The extent of Freeman's contribution to the apology finally made by Kevin Rudd to the Aboriginal people on 13 February 2008 will be much debated by sociologists and cultural experts. Sport likes to claim credit for major social changes, but the evidence is often less than conclusive. She herself has always downplayed her role in such major issues, preferring to concentrate, as she did on the track, on the practical rather than the poetic. 'I'm not about barriers, I'm not about racism,' she once said. 'I just take things in my stride. I always have.'

The one exception, perhaps, the one true driving force in her life, was the early death of Anne-Marie, her elder sister, who was born with cerebral palsy. Anne-Marie spent much of her life in a home for the disabled and died of an asthma attack in 1990 just three days before Freeman won her first gold at a major championships in the 4 x 100m Relay in Auckland. In her autobiography, Freeman remembers the chiding of her mother some mornings when bed seemed a more attractive option than training or school. 'You've got two good arms and two good legs, now go out there and use 'em.' The saying still makes Freeman laugh, but Anne-Marie's courage against adversity gave the words a particular poignancy.

After Sydney, Freeman took time off to come to terms

with her new status. She returned to the track in 2002 and led Australia to the gold medal in the 4 x 400m Relay at the Commonwealth Games in Manchester. But her heart was no longer in athletics. Her horizons had broadened and her job as a national icon was becoming full time.

Her real passion now is her own Catherine Freeman Foundation, which funds and organises educational and social projects in Palm Island. This paradise island, one of the original Aboriginal settlements, just off the coast of Queensland, is still striving to shake off massive social problems and years of neglect. The Foundation has given Freeman, now newly married and, at the time of writing, expecting her first child, a new purpose in life. To borrow a word from the Bahá'í Faith, it has created a 'oneness' between her past and her present. 'I was always running away from the limelight,' she said 10 years after that epic night in Sydney. 'Now, through the Foundation, I'm starting to embrace it.' If forging a brighter tomorrow for the people of Palm Island means talking about yesterday, then the price is worth paying. 'It's part of the same journey', she says. For the rest of us, that journey began and ended on a night when Stacy Dragila went on to win Olympic gold in the Pole Vault, Phillips Idowu finished a creditable sixth in the Triple Jump and Catherine Astrid Salome Freeman, for a beat under 50 seconds, united a nation.

Tanni's Golden Farewell

Athens 2004

Andrew Longmore

*At her fifth and last Paralympic Games, Britain's greatest
wheelchair racer bows out in style*

When it was all over, Tanni Grey-Thompson had nothing more left to give – not to the crowd at the Olympic
Stadium in Athens nor to the waiting BBC television cameras or to the press. Her overwhelming desire was to get
off the track as quickly as possible and be reunited with
her family, Ian, her husband and coach, and Carys, her little
daughter. She didn't do a lap of honour: she barely had
enough strength left to push herself over the line to win
the 400m, her second gold at these Paralympic Games
and her record-breaking 11th gold medal.

Statistically, at that moment, Tanni Grey-Thompson had
become the most decorated British athlete in Paralympic
history; emotionally, she was a shell. Though she did not
officially retire until nearly three years later, by the end of
Athens 2004 she knew her time was up. Her body was
saying 'enough' and her mind was starting to let in daylight. Only the date of departure needed red-lettering.
'Athletics has never been a choice for me,' she once said.
'As soon as it became a choice, I knew I shouldn't be
doing it anymore.'

Since her competitive debut in the Junior National Games in Cardiff in 1984, athletics had been an obsession, all-consuming, the one non-negotiable part of a life that had been lived in a wheelchair since the age of seven. Even Carys's birthdate was planned to fit her and her husband's championship schedule. But Athens had drained her, pushed her into the red, made her search so deep inside her soul for the last ounce of motivation and courage that the whole show, from the start of the 800m to overwhelming vindication in the 100m and ultimate triumph in the 400m, developed almost unwittingly into the curtain call for a great career. 'I don't think I've ever experienced so many emotions in such a short space of time,' she said.

It was a long time into her new life, a Damehood and a Baronetcy later perhaps, that she began to appreciate exactly what her husband meant when he'd said that winning all three golds in Athens would have been 'boring'. Reliving the emptiness of her defeat in the 800m still leaves her cold, but if she had not lost the race, supposedly her strongest discipline, so ineptly, let herself and others down so badly, would she have had the will, the sheer vengeful force, to win the 100m a few days later? And if victory in the 100m had not released a whole jack-in-the-box jumble of emotion, would she have remained as calm and composed for the 400m when the record 11th gold was so publicly at stake that the BBC had adapted their schedule to ensure it was broadcast on breakfast television?

But, back to the beginning, back to the start of the 800m and to the weird feeling of disengagement settling over the three-times Paralympic 800m champion. Preparations had gone well in the weeks before Athens; a few too many defeats had laced the record of an obsessive

winner and she had felt strangely lethargic in the demon-
stration race at the Olympic Games a month before, but
she thought she was ready. She had made a subtle, but
significant, technical change to her racing chair, increasing the size of the pushing rim to improve her starts. The
downside of the change was that she couldn't accelerate
as easily, which narrowed the tactical options for a punishing race such as the 800m. She needed to get a good
start, treat the first lap like a time trial and hang on for
dear life to the finish.

'So what did I do?' she recalled a few years on. 'I decided
to sit in the middle of the pack. I remember thinking, "heck,
what am I doing?" About 170 metres into the race I knew I
was screwed and I was. The pace we were going there was
no way I was going to get all the way round the field.'

The last lap was a miserable experience, a matter of
just getting to the end and counting the cost. She finished
seventh of eight. At the line, she had a heated exchange
with Ian, burst into tears and descended into a spiral of
misery and self-recrimination that reflected not, as some
thought, a lack of grace in defeat but her most basic fear:
she hadn't done herself justice. After all the preparation,
all the hours pounding the roads, she had just messed it
up and it didn't matter one bit that she had already won
the title in the T53 category three times, in the Paralympic
Games in Barcelona, Atlanta and Sydney. Her whole
life had been dedicated to winning and, as importantly,
to being allowed to lead her life the way she wanted to.
Now she had just been horribly human and blown it all
away. At least that's what it felt like until she returned to
the bosom of her family and asked Carys whether she
had seen Mummy racing. 'No,' replied her two-year-old
daughter, 'I had a hot dog.'

The nagging concern for Grey-Thompson was that she had seen the defeat coming. In the call room before the race, she had been nervous as ever, but somehow disconnected, almost unbothered. She had never felt so empty before a race. Unwittingly Phil Jones, the BBC interviewer, began the process of recovery by asking the tough question. Was this a Paralympic Games too far for a 35-year-old? Had he been less direct with his interrogation, shown a glimpse of pity or sympathy, Grey-Thompson reflected, she might have sunk even lower than she did. She also might have hit him. But the very legitimacy of the question shocked her. No, of course not. 'When the interview had finished, Phil just gave me a huge hug and I remember just clinging on to him for dear life because he'd been so nice to me,' says Grey-Thompson.

When she did retire from international competition, at Manchester in spring 2007, Grey-Thompson organised a dinner. It was a dinner to celebrate her extraordinary career, but also to say thank you to a select group of people who did not necessarily know what they'd done to help. Two people on the guest list that night were Jenny Ridley, a long-time friend and training partner, and Francesca Porcellato, an Italian athlete and rival. Ridley had been flying in the lead-up to the 2004 Paralympic Games, but a doubt had emerged about her eligibility to compete and she had to withdraw from the Games at the last moment. On the morning after the 800m, Ridley was still there to accompany Grey-Thompson on a training push. 'That was an incredible gesture,' Tanni reflects. 'We'd spent a lot of time crying together for all sorts of reasons. She was strong and fit and fast but she couldn't even compete. It must have been so painful for her.'

Porcellato's support was equally generous and utterly

spontaneous. On the warm-up track before the 100m, Grey-Thompson threw up 12 times. Even for her, this was a world record. She would have done anything to have raced the 400m after the 800m; instead, she was pitched into the 100m, probably her least favoured event. Husband Ian, who was coach to the whole GB wheelchair squad, including Tanni, had been told to keep away in the warm-up area so another coach was deputed to hold bags of ice onto the back of Tanni's neck. The evening was warm and the Stadium was alive. Grey-Thompson, by her own admission, was terrified. 'Are you OK?' came the familiar Italian lilt of Porcellato. 'Don't worry, Tanni, you're going to have a good day today. I know it.'

It wasn't much of an exchange but it made Grey-Thompson feel a lot better. She wouldn't have done anything to destabilise the Italian, but she admits she wouldn't have been able to offer such unqualified support to Porcellato if the roles had been reversed. 'She's a friend, but, at that moment, she was a rival,' Grey-Thompson says. 'I thanked her much later and she just looked a bit embarrassed. I don't think she knew what I was talking about.'

In the Stadium, Grey-Thompson was so determined and focussed that she did not warm up with the rest of the field. She just sat and watched the clock tick down. When the race began, Porcellato scorched into an early lead. But Grey-Thompson had promised herself that, whatever happened, unlike the 800m, she wouldn't panic and she stayed true to her word. The British athlete caught the Italian at 60m but at the line barely a few inches of daylight separated the two wheelchairs. The race lasted just over 17 seconds, but it seemed like a lifetime to the winner, whose exuberant celebrations mixed relief with atonement and joy. The first person to congratulate her was Francesca Porcellato. That race was perfection, said Grey-Thompson, who is not given to exaggeration about her own performances. 'It was the most emotional race I've ever run,' she says. 'I wouldn't swap it for anything.'

With the 10th gold safely stashed away, the 400m was a relative breeze. Records never really meant much to Grey-Thompson, but she happily played the game to keep the media interested. At least that's her story. The 400m was scheduled for the ninth day of the Games initially, under an agreement reached between the organisers and the BBC, who wanted to show each one of Tanni's races in a prime-time evening slot. But the race was postponed until the morning of the 10th day, 27 September. Privately, Grey-Thompson was relieved that her record-breaking attempt would be a more private affair. Then Colin Jackson came bounding across to tell her that the race was going to be broadcast live on *BBC Breakfast*. 'Aren't you pleased?' he asked, noticing the rather subdued reaction.

No one need have worried, not the viewers nor Grey-Thompson herself. With the fast-starting Porcellato conveniently stationed on her outside to drag her through the first quarter of the race, Grey-Thompson knew there would be no repeat of her dawdling in the 800m. Her one concern was the fast late finish of the Swede, Madelene Nordlund. Grey-Thompson, though, had the race won by the home turn and, despite the build-up of lactic acid in her shoulders, pushed on to a handsome victory, with the luckless Porcellato again taking silver. There was none of the electricity of the 100m success; the setting, early morning in an echoing Stadium, did not deserve it. 'I felt really happy inside, but I was struggling to show it,' she says.

Grey-Thompson dislikes the phrase 'triumph over

adversity', often applied to Paralympic excellence. There's not much adversity in the life of a Paralympic athlete, she says, at least not compared with the ordinary wheelchair user who has to catch a bus to work every day or negotiate the London Underground. Her childhood in a quiet suburb of Cardiff was conditioned by parents who fought tooth and nail to get equal opportunities for their oldest child, who had suffered from spina bifida from birth, but who fostered her independence with equal care. Tanni's father, Peter, was an architect, but he didn't remodel the house to make it easier for Tanni. 'We had to give Tanni the chance to live in the real world,' he once explained. And the real world was a tough place – much tougher, Grey-Thompson reckons, than the racetrack.

Now Baroness Grey-Thompson of Eaglescliffe, a crossbencher in the House of Lords, has set her sights on wider goals. Her diary is brimful of talks, dinners, appearances, committees and meetings which all have to be fitted round her daily duties in the Upper House. She is a member of the Board of London Transport and of UK Athletics and patron of a number of charities. She still trains, still races occasionally, but her competitive career turned a full circle during those eight days at Athens 2004. At the end of it, athletics was no longer her whole life. It was time to take on the real world.

Barefoot out of Africa

Rome 1960
Tom Knight

On a starlit evening in the Eternal City, Abebe Bikila won the Marathon and carried the torch for a new continent

The slight, upright figure in a green vest and red shorts was still shrouded in darkness on the Appian Way and as he ran powerfully towards them, the journalists gathered in the temporary stands at the finish of the Marathon thought they had misheard the on-course commentator. That was because the name of the runner fast approaching the finish line meant nothing to them. But this was Abebe Bikila and the hitherto unknown Ethiopian was on his way to making history as the first Sub-Saharan African to win an Olympic Games title.

The British journalist Neil Allen was among those waiting at the finish. In his *Olympic Diary: Rome 1960*, he recalled: 'We thought we'd misheard the name of an athlete when, at 1000m to go, we were told that Abebe Bikila was going to win the Marathon. Suddenly, we could see the lights of a little convoy twinkling in the distance ... and here he came, trotting rhythmically and strongly up the Appian Way.'

Moments before breasting the tape stretched across the road under the floodlit Arch of Constantine, Bikila raised his hands only slightly and certainly not enough to suggest any celebration for a victory that was met with shock and wonderment by all those who were there. The toughest event in the Olympic Games schedule, run for the first time at night and with a start and finish outside the main Stadium, had been won in emphatic style by an unknown athlete who had dared take to the streets of Rome – cobbles and all – in bare feet. With a calm efficiency belying his background and lack of sporting pedigree, he had then proceeded to cover the 26.2 miles in 2:15:16, a time that wiped almost eight minutes off the great Emil Zátopek's Helsinki 1952 record and faster than any man had covered the distance before. This by a 28-year-old international novice running – seemingly effortlessly – through the ancient streets of the city from where the dictator, Benito Mussolini, had launched Italy's invasion of Ethiopia some 25 years previously.

The symbolism of Bikila's triumph and the fact that Bikila had made his decisive move at 40km, as they passed the Ethiopian obelisk of Axum, looted on Mussolini's orders by the invading Italian soldiers, was not immediately reflected in his modest reaction at the finish. There was no jumping around, no whoops of delight from Bikila, whose serenity at his moment of triumph baffled the Italian officials. They offered him a blanket but this was waved away as Bikila took in the scene, touched his toes and jogged on the spot. The spell was broken only when his coach, Onni Niskanen, the former soldier and adventurer from Sweden who had masterminded the presence of Ethiopia's 15-strong team at these Games, rushed from the sidelines to hug Bikila. The new champion looked around, taking in the effect his performance had produced and laughed until the joy was washed away by his tears of relief. When Rhadi Ben Abdesselam, an accomplished athlete and a pre-race favourite from Morocco, came through the line, Bikila paused his celebrations to pat him on the back. The pair had run side-by-side, accompanied only by their own shadows cast by the flares lighting the route, from the 18th kilometre and Bikila would later refer to Ben Abdesselam as 'that stubborn Moroccan'. Asked why he had run without shoes, Bikila replied through an interpreter, 'I wanted the world to know that my country Ethiopia has always won with determination and heroism.'

Later still and Bikila, now dressed in an official Ethiopian tracksuit, stood on top of the podium to receive his historic gold medal – the last of those Olympic Games – and shake hands with Ben Abdesselam and Barry Magee, the New Zealander who came third. A brief medical examination after the race showed Bikila to be in tremendous condition, with a pulse of only 88bpm and no signs of any damage to the blackened soles of his now-famous feet. It later emerged that he had arrived in Rome with a pair of running shoes that were too worn out to compete in. Together with his teammates, Bikila went shopping for a new pair. These he wore for a couple of days, but the poor fit left him with blisters. It was only in the last few days before the race that he decided to run barefoot, just as he used to do at home.

If some of the 69 runners who had lined up at the start on Capitol Hill had sniggered at the sight of Bikila's bare feet, they, like the rest of the world, were forced to take a fresh look at what constituted a top class Marathon runner at the start of the 1960s. Mel Watman, a doyen of the world's athletics writers, was on leave from his RAF National Service and at his first Olympic Games in Rome, covering the event for *Athletics Weekly*. He said: 'There was a serenity about Bikila. He seemed to float along. Everyone had to revise their thinking after what he did in Rome. His victory remains one of the most significant performances in athletics history. He beat the best in the world and set a new world record. It was the start of a whole new era in distance running which continues to this day.'

Amid yet more drama, Bikila returned to the Olympic Games four years later in Tokyo and, this time wearing shoes, became the first man to retain the Marathon title with another world record, only 40 days after undergoing an appendectomy. But he will always be remembered for that night in Rome, where distance running was not alone in experiencing the start of a new era. Rome 1960 were the Olympic Games of Herb Elliott, Livio Berruti, Wilma Rudolph and Rafer Johnson on the track as well as the charismatic Cassius Clay in the Boxing ring, yet there was so much about the Rome 1960 Games that highlighted major changes in the world, in sport and beyond the five Olympic Rings. The USA was not its usual dominant force on the track and there was a greater array of medallists than ever before.

Within months of the Rome 1960 Games ending, the unveiling of the Berlin Wall meant that East and West Germany would not compete again as a single nation until Barcelona 1992. Most significantly, the Rome Games were the first to be beamed across the world by television, thanks to broadcasting agreements signed by the Italian National Olympic Committee with CBS in the United States and Eurovision for the rest of Europe. Further agreements with NHK in Japan meant the Rome 1960 Games were seen in 21 countries. What people saw on television was a stylish, vibrant Rome at the start of the 1960s, in the midst of the so-called 'economic miracle'. Organisers made sure that the city became a major feature of the Games, illuminating the architecture at night with flares and spotlights.

When discussing Bikila's victory, Neil Allen's *Olympic Diary* cited Pliny's 'Always something new out of Africa'. This quote is often used today in athletics because exciting talents regularly emerge from that continent, but in 1960 it was unheard of outside the white-dominated South Africa. Bikila, born in Jatto, no more than a collection of dwellings some three hours' drive from the Ethiopian capital, Addis Ababa, was brought up the son of peasant farmers and became used to running barefoot as he minded the family's animals. He followed his mother to the capital in 1951 and a year later joined the Imperial Bodyguard, the troops charged with protecting Emperor Haile Selassie. He played football, volleyball and basketball, but took to athletics when he was picked out by Niskanen, who had been recruited as the Guard's sports coach. In *Bikila, Ethiopia's Barefoot Olympian*, Tim Judah describes how in late-1956 Niskanen had noticed Bikila running daily from Sululta, where he was living, to Addis and back and thought he should try the Marathon. For Bikila, the Marathon was the chance to travel abroad and emulate those Ethiopians who had been the first to represent their country at Melbourne 1956.

In Bikila, Niskanen quickly saw an immense talent and the pair became very close as athlete and coach. He ran only two Marathons before the Games and both were in Ethiopia. The second of them, a trial race, secured his selection for Rome and his winning time of 2:21:23 – inside the world record – would have alerted the world to his potential had the news leaked out of Ethiopia. Even when journalists in Rome were told about this performance, the overriding reaction was disbelief: the course must have been short or the timing inaccurate. So it was that Bikila and his teammates arrived in Rome with the Ethiopian authorities still sceptical about the cost of it all following the country's failure to win anything in Melbourne.

After Rome, of course, Bikila returned to Ethiopia as a national hero and huge crowds, whipped up by the media, surged to the airport in Addis to greet his arrival, despite the fact that, even then, many Ethiopians were more interested in football than athletics. A cavalcade took Bikila to the Imperial Palace, where the Emperor presented him with the Star of Ethiopia and promoted him to the rank of Corporal.

The four years between Rome 1960 and Tokyo 1964 saw Bikila feted wherever he went. His fame was a factor in him escaping censure following the failed coup by Imperial Guardsmen in late 1960. He won races around the world, including the 1961 Mainichi Marathon in Osaka, where he was presented with his first pair of custom-made running shoes because the President of the Onitsuka Tiger company – later to become Asics – warned him against running barefoot on Japan's rough roads. Kihachiro Onitsuka had watched Bikila win in Rome and was determined to see the Olympic champion in his own brand of shoes. Despite Bikila's scepticism about the value of shoes, Onitsuka took his measurements and within a couple of days had produced the trainers in which he went on to win the Marathon in front of crowds a million-strong along the route. The cast for the shoes has been saved for posterity at the Asics headquarters in Kobe and in the Olympic Museum in Lausanne. Onitsuka, who died, aged 89 in 2007, repeated the story to me in 1992 and his meeting with Bikila remained one of his finest memories.

Bikila's attempt at a third Olympic Games victory ended when injury forced him to pull out after 17km of the 1968 Marathon in Mexico City, where his long-time training partner, Mamo Wolde, succeeded him as champion.

Abebe Bikila's life changed forever on the night of 22 March 1969, when his car spun off the road as he returned to Addis. He was in a coma for four days. His injuries were so severe that doctors predicted he would never walk again and the Emperor insisted that he should be transferred to England and the specialist treatment available at Stoke Mandeville Hospital in Buckinghamshire.

Confined to a wheelchair, Bikila was reportedly a model patient and spent eight months at Stoke Mandeville. As a celebrity patient, he was even visited by the Queen as he underwent rehabilitation. His treatment included being introduced to the world of sport for the disabled. In the hospital that spawned the modern Paralympic Movement, Bikila took up archery and, in 1970, returned to England to take part in the Stoke Mandeville Games. In 1971, he competed in archery and table tennis at a disabled games in Norway and even finished first in a sleigh-riding race. As a guest of honour at Munich 1972, he shook the hand of the newly crowned Marathon champion, Frank Shorter. Bikila died from a brain haemorrhage in 1973, aged 41.

There are statues, buildings and awards all over the world in Bikila's honour and images of him running so effortlessly were used in the 1976 John Schlesinger-directed movie, *Marathon Man*. The running revolution Bikila headed has seen Ethiopian athletes win 18 gold medals at the Olympic Games and East Africans dominate distance running in events around the globe. The most famous of Bikila's successors is Haile Gebrselassie, who has twice won Olympic gold at 10,000m but has yet to achieve his ultimate ambition of winning the Marathon. For Gebrselassie, who was born in the year that Bikila died, the legacy of the barefoot Marathon champion lives on. He told *Time* magazine: 'Before Abebe Bikila, there were no runners in Africa, or at least no runners that the world knew about. After Bikila won the Marathon at Rome 1960, we Africans all started thinking: "Look – he is one of us. If he can do it, we can do the same." Now there are thousands of us, winning races all over the world, setting new standards and breaking records. In one of my offices, there is a poster that shows all the great champions Ethiopia has produced. Bikila is there right in the centre. He is an icon for the whole of Africa, and a personal hero of mine. If it weren't for him, I would still be a farmer in the hills of Arsi.'

Thunderbolt and Lightning

Beijing 2008

Paul Hayward

*How a 1.95m Jamaican changed the face of sprinting …
in just 9.69 seconds*

In sport all kinds of hyperbolic claims are made on behalf of triumphs that turn out to be transitory, but the 100m retains an advantage. It stands as a measure of human evolution – of the potential improvability of Homo sapiens – and in Beijing one summer night in 2008 that measure flashed straight past us in the shape of Usain Bolt.

The ornate Bird's Nest Stadium was an architectural statement of Chinese know-how and power. It had laid on many delights before the field for the Olympic 100m Final twitched and fidgeted on the starting line. The Beijing 2008 Olympic Games were progressing in a vast compound, built by China to confirm their emergence as an economic superpower, to designate this as the Chinese century. The crowd had been engaged, curious, obedient and noisy in an ordered kind of way. Not until Bolt hunkered down in lane four, though, did the Bird's Nest lose control. Only then did involuntary awe seize China's Games.

The 100m is unique. Olympic competition distils varied themes into one sub-10-second frenzy. Men and women train for weeks, months, years, to achieve the quickest possible coronation. Part of Bolt's appeal, however, was that you could barely imagine him training at all, such was his weakness for chicken nuggets, his agreeably relaxed demeanour.

Here was an athlete built for 200m–400m running, not the power-packed eruption of the 100m dash. A whole generation of sprinters had conformed to a pattern of squat, muscle-bound speed. Bolt was leggy, lithe, fluid, not staccato in his steps. Most of all he was tall at 1.95m, elegant, athletically versatile in a way the human cannon-balls who preceded him had not been.

The moment of truth came one muggy night, at a Games that were proceeding with great order but rather less emotion from the audience. Bolt was one of three Jamaicans who started down the Bird's Nest track to the sprinters' moment of realisation: the Olympic gold, now a guarantee of vast celebrity and wealth.

Bolt wore No. 2163, a curiously random and high fig-ure for the obvious nonpareil of straight-line running. In May 2008 in New York, 'Lightning Bolt' had lowered the world record to 9.72 at the Reebok Grand Prix. He was already the world's fastest man. But an Olympic final is a whole new maelstrom of pressure. Even in the best, sometimes, muscles can lock, breathing can tighten, and the whole drama can invade the head, with disastrous consequences.

For 40m, when the gun sounded (and when the pis-tol goes off, you are soon 40m into the race, the speed these men go), Bolt seemed to have fallen prey to these ruinous expectations. He was in the leading group, but merely keeping pace rather than attacking the field as a champion must. It was here that we saw the extraordin-ary mechanics of his body in their clearest form. With no discernible change from coasting to exploding, Bolt was suddenly high-stepping away from his rivals as if they were figures in a painting.

In the NBC recording, we hear the commentator exclaim: 'Usain Bolt, sprinting ahead, winning by daylight!' This was the second when a single individual sped away from the rest of humanity. The gap opened up by Bolt on Richard Thompson, who took silver, was a marvel of science that expressed the gulf between good and special. Bolt might have been met at the line by people in white laboratory coats, and taken away for scientific study, because his surge brought not only a personal victory but also a human leap. Never has the 100m world record been broken so spectacularly, or with such a dramatic effect on a live audience.

Why? Because Bolt 'stopped running', according to the NBC commentator, 20m from the line. Later that was exposed as an exaggeration. A better estimate was 15m out. Yet the fact of Bolt's showboating was indisputable. First he looked round for Powell, his closest rival. Then, realising he was out on his own, beyond catching, he dropped his arms to his side and started celebrating, slapping his chest with his palm before dancing over the line in 9.69, adjusted from 9.683. Another glorious detail: one of Bolt's shoelaces was untied. It at least made it easier for him to remove them when he placed them, like museum exhibits, on the track.

How fast might he have run without the self-congratulatory cabaret at the end? On the basis of the first 60m Bolt's coach claimed his winning time could have been 9.52. Later the Institute of Theoretical Astrophysics at the University of Oslo also calculated a sub-9.60 time. In all these moments, one assumes no one will ever run faster – that the end of the line has been reached. One word answers that: Berlin. But more of that later.

In the crowd, in the press box and the International Olympic Committee enclosures, time, which had run so fast for Bolt's rampage, seemed to stop, as each witness took a few beats of the heart to absorb what they had seen. This is the private moment offered by all great sporting events. Each observer is allowed to record and assess in a personal sphere an achievement that is at once global, universal, and at the same time particular to the spectator.

All top acts need a catchphrase, or a gesture, and Bolt's was to pull his imaginary bow and fire a gilded arrow into the Beijing night. NBC's commentator enthused, 'The 100m may be run in a straight line, but Usain Bolt just turned the corner. They [Olympic sprinters] have now gone into the realm of video game times.' At trackside, later, Bolt was reminded by an American TV reporter that this was his first season as a 100m runner. 'I'm just happy,' Bolt kept saying, over and over, without emotion. We were shocked by his brilliance. He, quite obviously, was not. 'I was slowing down long before the finish and wasn't tired at all,' he said later. 'I could have gone back to the start and done it all over again.'

Before he could make it to the media inquisition in the deepest chambers of the Stadium, Bolt had family and fans to attend to. Over on the far side of the Bird's Nest a recording was made of Bolt's mother, Jennifer, rejoicing. The sound she made was a kind of ecstatic, incredulous screaming. To be Usain 'Lightning Bolt' was one thing. But imagine being his mother. Fancy going home that night knowing you had given birth to the world's fastest man, the star of China's first Olympics.

The son threw himself into the arms of the mother, over

the hoardings, as other Jamaican team members celebrated with them. Caught in the melee were two Chinese
spectators, rendered delirious by their proximity to such
an astounding story. Their giddiness was the perfect context for Bolt's more urbane joy. They were the host country
allowing itself to get carried away by the human spectacle, rather than the impressive scale of the construction
project or the 'message' these Games sent out to the rest
of the world. As he pulled away from the throng, Bolt held
out a Jamaican flag, above and behind his head, to mark
this out as a victory for a Caribbean community outside
the mainstream of heavily funded sport.

In the BBC commentary booth, Michael Johnson, the
great 200m–400m flier, asked: 'When has anyone ever
shut down on people in the Olympic 100m Final? He is a
global superstar now.'

In the newspaper world, thoughts would have turned,
even 10 years ago, to the crafting of a report for the following day's publication, but by 2008 the Internet was
king, adding frenzy to the filing of dispatches. This story
was happening now, not on tomorrow's inky pages. The
media worked ever faster to allow people around the
world to digest the wonder they had witnessed within minutes, not hours, of Bolt partying across the line.

Soon the miracle of Bolt's run was mutating into a
discussion about his celebratory routine and the wasted
opportunity to lower his own world record even further. Bolt himself offered an intriguing answer. His mission, he said, had been to win Olympic gold, for himself
and Jamaica, not to race the clock, which he could do
any time. Jacques Rogge, the IOC President, who is no
fogey and is not soundbite addicted, felt moved to scold
Bolt for his conduct over the last 15m–20m. He called

the showboating 'disrespectful' to the other beaten final-ists. Bolt drew his bow and fired back: 'I wasn't bragging. When I saw I wasn't covered, I was just happy.' Edmund Bartlett, a Jamaican government minister, took his part declaring, 'We have to see it in the glory of their moment and give it to them. We have to allow the personality of youth to express itself.'

Bolt's was a specifically Jamaican triumph, a coun-terpoint to the expensive, driven exploits of a generation of American sprinters. When the issue of performance enhancing substances was raised in the minutes after Bolt's romp, it was claimed that a generation of non-American speedsters had merely stepped into the void created by the illegal dominance of the Tim Montgomery/ Justin Gatlin era. In other words, smaller nations were now being allowed to compete on a level track.

Spectators had earned the right, by then, to retain a measure of scepticism about any superhuman feat in ath-letics. Yet the prevailing sense there in the vast amphi-theatre was that Bolt's conquest should be greeted as a legitimate phenomenon until or unless there was evidence to the contrary.

It was certainly a victory for grass-roots sport, in clubs and schools. Born in August 1986 to grocer parents near Trelawny, Jamaica, Bolt excelled at cricket and football before demonstrating potential as a runner at Waldensia school, where he represented his parish in national cham-pionships. At high school coaches attempted to curb his casual approach to training and love of practical jokes. The combination of languid and mischievous character-ised his journey all the way to Beijing and right down the 100m track.

In every act in China, Bolt was being true to his nature

while opening a window on the potent athletic culture of his island, which experienced a golden run in the Olympic Stadium. The 100m was only the first stage in his Beijing blast, which explains the coolness of his demeanour in the subsequent press conferences. He responded to questions in clichés and monosyllables and soon wearied of the ritual. But he did confirm chicken nuggets as his favoured fuel. The world saw an end-of-the-rainbow tale, but by then Bolt was looking down the 200m course as well. The final of that longer race was four days away. In Bolt's head, you could see, the story had already moved on.

Carl Lewis had set the template for sprinters coveting the 100m–200m sprint double, at Los Angeles in 1984. Now there was also Johnson's historic world 200m record to hone in on: 19.32, set at Atlanta 1996. Johnson believed this magical figure would survive a Bolt lightning strike. He said: 'I don't think his training has given him enough speed endurance but eventually it will and then I will be able to kiss my record goodbye. I don't think he will break it here.'

Don Quarrie, the Jamaican sprinter who won gold in the 200m at Montreal 1976, thought otherwise, and was right. Bolt crossed the line in 19.30, despite the headwind, and became the first since Quarrie to hold the world 100m and 200m records simultaneously. 'I blew my mind. I blew the world's mind,' the new champion proclaimed. 'I've been saying all season that the 200m means a lot more to me than the 100m. I knew I could run that fast. I told myself – if I'm going to get that world record, it's going to be here because it's a fast track.'

This time Bolt raced the clock as well, and charged all the way to the line, to be greeted by a tannoy rendition of 'Happy Birthday' to mark his arrival, at midnight, at 22 years of age. His final flourish at China's Games was to run the third-leg of the Jamaican 4 x 100m Relay team (Powell ran fourth) to complete his trio of golds, then donate $50,000 to the Sichuan earthquake relief effort.

Now the postscript. A year to the day after his globe-grabbing exploits in China's capital, Bolt lowered his 100m Beijing mark to 9.58, shaving 11-hundredths of a second off his Olympic record time, at the World Championships in Berlin, on Jesse Owens' stage. In the 96 years the International Association of Athletics Federations has kept records no sprinter has improved the world's best 100m time by such a large margin in one step.

The best human speed over the 100m had fallen from 10.6 in 1912 to 9.58 in 2009, less than 100 years later. The next day Bolt broke his own 200m world record, completing the set of world and Olympic sprinting titles, in 19.19, despite claiming to be 'tired'.

Bolt blamed his car crash in April for his inability to run even faster. Of the 100m, he said, 'Now I plan to do even better in the future. I could go 9.4, but I think the world stops at 9.4.' So in a narrow sense the miracle of the Beijing Olympic Games lasted only a year, but the context was everything. That night, at a Games where political and economic power shifted east, and a sprinter from a country of 2.8m people showed us a more thrilling kind of progress.

Contributors

Kate Battersby became the first female chief sports writer in Fleet Street, in 1996, on the *Evening Standard*. She has also worked across a variety of sports as a feature writer, reporter and columnist for a number of national newspapers, including *The Daily Telegraph*, *The Sunday Telegraph* and *The Sunday Times*.

Gareth A Davies is an award-winning sports writer who has been Paralympics Correspondent for The Telegraph Media Group at the last four Paralympic Games. The International Paralympic Committee bestowed the prestigious 'World Print Media Coverage Award' to *The Daily Telegraph* after its coverage of the 2004 Games, and to *The Sunday Telegraph* after the 2008 Games. Davies was at the heart of *The Telegraph*'s coverage.

Barry Davies will be commentating on his 12th Olympic Games in 2012. He has also covered eight Olympic Winter Games, 11 football World Cups, seven European football Championships and nine Commonwealth Games. He began his television career with ITV, commentating on the World Cup in 1966 and the Mexico City 1968 Olympic Games two years later. He worked in the BBC Sports department from 1969 until 2004, and is now a freelance writer. He has commentated on many different sports including athletics, badminton, figure skating, gymnastics, hockey, tennis (27 Wimbledon Championships) and the Boat Race. Barry was awarded an MBE in 2005.

Brendan Gallagher is the chief sports feature writer at *The Daily Telegraph*, specialising in basketball, rugby, cycling, athletics and cricket. He has co-authored the autobiography of Ireland and Lions captain Brian O'Driscoll and, most recently, of three times Olympic gold medal winner Bradley Wiggins, *In Pursuit of Glory*. A former director of Hayters Sports Agency, he has a particular interest in historical sporting events and the Olympic and Paralympic Games heritage.

Doug Gillon has spent more than 40 happy years as a sports writer. He has reported on more than 60 sports from over 40 countries and covered 10 Summer Olympics and 10 Commonwealth Games, most of them as athletics correspondent of *The Herald*. An erstwhile Scottish Schoolboys steeplechase champion, he has twice been SJA regional sports writer of the year as well as SJA specialist writer – the first from outside Fleet Street. Past chair of the British Athletics Writers' Association, he has claimed numerous Scottish awards, including winning his considerable weight in whisky (85 bottles of Scotch).

John Goodbody will be covering the 2012 Olympic Games for *The Sunday Times*, his 12th successive Summer Games. He is the author of four books on the Games. John was sports news correspondent of *The Times* (1986–2007), winning awards in all three decades on the paper, including being Sports Reporter of the Year in 2001. As a competitor, he broke British junior weightlifting records, was a member of the national judo squad, and became Cambridge University's No1 shot-putter. In 1991, aged 48, he became the oldest Briton for 18 years to swim the English Channel.

Paul Hayward is chief sports writer for the *Observer*. He has collaborated with Sir Bobby Robson and Michael Owen on their autobiographies. Paul has covered four Olympic Games and five World Cups, among other major sporting events. He is a regular contributor to Sky Sports' Sunday Supplement and has written documentary scripts for BBC television. He has twice been named Sports Writer of the Year in the British Press Awards.

Murray Hedgcock is a London-based Australian journalist who covered a range of sports primarily for the national daily, *The Australian*. Born in Melbourne, he worked on provincial dailies before coming to England in 1953 with the aim of watching Hassett's Ashes tourists in action. After two years on a London suburban paper, he returned to Australia, and joined the Murdoch organisation at *The News* in Adelaide. He was posted to the News Limited London bureau in 1966 and spent 15 years as bureau chief. After taking early retirement in 1991, he became a consultant to News International.

Tom Knight has worked in journalism for 30 years and covered eight Olympic Games, 10 World Athletics Championships and four Commonwealth Games. He was *The Daily Telegraph*'s athletics correspondent for 10 years and was a member of SJA award-winning 'top team in sports journalism' (2004) who campaigned in support of the London 2012 Olympic bid. Tom has contributed to *The Times, Guardian, Independent, Mail on Sunday, Daily Express* and the Press Association, and has appeared as an Olympic Games observer and athletics expert on Radio 2, Radio 5 Live, Talksport, Channel 4 and CNN.

Craig Lord is a sports writer for *The Times* and *Sunday Times* and the senior correspondent for the specialist publication *SwimNews*. A former Deputy Editor of *Times Online*, he masterminded the Sydney Olympic Games online microsite for *The Times*. He has reported on the past five Olympic Games for the London-based news organisation. In 2007, Lord received the Al Schoenfield Media Award from the International Swimming Hall of Fame and in 2009 he was presented with the American Swimming Coaches Association Media Award.

Kevin McCallum is the chief sports writer of *The Star* newspaper in Johannesburg, where he has lived since his family emigrated to South Africa from Northern Ireland when he was 10. He has covered the Paralympic and Olympic Games, and the Commonwealth Games, as well as rugby, cricket and football World Cups. He has twice been named as the country's top sports columnist and feature writer of the year, and in 2002 won the South African Sports Writer of the Year award. He has written two best-selling books on South African cricket and sports trivia. London 2012 will be his third Olympic Games, and he will cover the Paralympic Games for the fourth time in 2012.

David Miller has been a sports writer for more than 50 years, working as chief football correspondent for the *Daily Telegraph* and *Sunday Telegraph* from 1960–1973, then as chief sports writer for *The Express* (1973–1982) and *The Times* (1982–97). He has covered 14 Football World Cups and 20 Winter and Summer Olympic Games. In 2001, he won the SJA's Doug Gardner trophy for his services to sports journalism. He has also written 21 books, including biographies of Sir Matt Busby, Sebastian Coe and Juan Antonio Samaranch.

Nick Townsend was a *Daily Mail* sports writer for many years before joining the *Independent on Sunday* as football correspondent. He later became the paper's chief sports writer. He is now a freelance, working primarily for *The Sunday Times*. As an author, he has collaborated with Sir Steve Redgrave and Ben Ainslie on their autobiographies.

Neil Wilson is the Olympic and athletics correspondent of the *Daily Mail*. He has covered every Summer Olympic Games since 1972 and the Winter Games since 1984. He has worked as a sports journalist for more than 40 years, reporting major events as diverse as the 1966 football World Cup, Wimbledon and the Boat Race. He was chosen Sports Journalist of the Year in the 1984 British Press Awards. He was editor of the British Olympic Association's official report of the 1976 Olympic Games and has written nine books on sporting themes.

Index